DISCARDED

FRAMES
OF REFERENTS

FRAMES OF REFERENTS

The Postmodern Poetry
of Guillermo Carnero

Jill Kruger-Robbins

Lewisburg
Bucknell University Press
London: Associated University Presses

© 1997 by Associated University Presses, Inc.

All rights reserved. Authorization to photocopy items for internal or personal use, or the internal or personal use of specific clients, is granted by the copyright owner, provided that a base fee of $10.00, plus eight cents per page, per copy is paid directly to the Copyright Clearance Center, 222 Rosewood Drive, Danvers, Massachusetts 01923. [0-8387-5327-2 $10.00 + 8¢ pp, pc.]

Associated University Presses
440 Forsgate Drive
Cranbury, NJ 08512

Associated University Presses
16 Barter Street
London WC1A 2AH, England

Associated University Presses
P.O. Box 338, Port Credit
Mississauga, Ontario
Canada L5G 4L8

The paper used in this publication meets the requirements of the American National Standard for Permanence of Paper for Printed Library Materials Z39.48-1984.

Library of Congress Cataloging-in-Publication Data

Kruger-Robbins, Jill, 1962–
    Frames of referents : The postmodern poetry of Guillermo Carnero / Jill Kruger-Robbins.
       p. cm.
    Includes bibliographical references (p.   ) and index.
    ISBN 0-8387-5327-2 (alk. paper)
    1. Carnero, Guillermo, 1947– —Criticism and interpretation. I. Title.
PQ6653.A68Z77   1997
861'.4—dc20
                                         96-25907
                                            CIP

PRINTED IN THE UNITED STATES OF AMERICA

For my parents,
with love and gratitude.

Contents

Acknowledgments	9
Introduction: The *Novísimos*, Postmodernism and the Poetry of Guillermo Carnero	13
1. Framing the Self in *Dibujo de la muerte*	29
2. A Question of Authority: *El sueño de Escipión*	51
3. Forms of Repetition: *Variaciones y figuras sobre un tema de La Bruyère*	76
4. Critical Paranoia: *El azar objetivo*	95
5. In Retrospect: *Divisibilidad indefinida*	116
Afterword	135
Notes	137
Bibliography	148
Index	155

Acknowledgments

I am enormously indebted to Guillermo Carnero, not only for his poetry and criticism but also for the time he has generously spent answering my queries in letters and in interviews both in Alicante and at Florida Atlantic University. I also thank him for graciously granting me permission to quote from his work, including the poems of *Dibujo de la muerte, El sueño de Escipión, Variaciones y figuras sobre un tema de La Bruyère, El azar objetivo,* and *Divisibilidad indefinida,* as well as from the essay "El juego lúgubre: la aportación de Salvador Dalí al pensamiento surrealista" from his book, *Las armas abisinias: Ensayos sobre literatura y arte del siglo XX.*

Guillermo Carnero's works are reprinted with permission of the editors. I thank Hiperión for allowing me to reprint poems from the second edition of *Ensayo de una teoría de la visión (Poesía, 1966–1977).* I am grateful to Renacimiento for permission to quote from *Divisibilidad indefinida (1979–1989)* and to Anthropos for allowing me to reprint passages of "El juego lúgubre."

All of the translations of Carnero's poetry in this book are my own. In all cases, I have attempted to preserve those poetic effects that are central to my analyses. Thus, I maintain the structural disposition of the texts because metonymical connections are occasionally made purely on the basis of the spatial contiguity of words and images. In the case of *Divisibilidad indefinida,* I maintain the stanzaic divisions, but I do not attempt to translate the Spanish sonnets into English sonnet form.

Versions of chapters 1 and 5 have appeared as articles in scholarly journals. I am grateful to Mary S. Vásquez for granting me permission to include a version of "Allusion, Metonymy, and the Speaker in Guillermo Carnero's *Dibujo de la muerte,*" *Letras Peninsulares* 8, no. 2 (1995): 261–77. Thanks as well go to Luis González-del-Valle for his permission to include a version of "The Shattered Image: Referentiality and the Speaker in Guillermo Carnero's *Divisibilidad indefinida*," *Anales de la Literatura Española Contemporánea* 20, nos. 1–2 (1995): 133–48.

I am also grateful to the Schmidt College of Arts and Humanities of Florida Atlantic University for a Schmidt Summer Fellowship in 1994, which allowed me to complete the initial manuscript of this book.

Several individuals supported me intellectually and emotionally throughout this project, and I wish to thank them here. I am most grateful to Andrew P. Debicki for his guidance in the early formulation of this project and for his unfailing encouragement and support. Thanks to Michael J. Doudoroff and Robert C. Spires for painstakingly reading and critiquing the manuscript at various stages of its development. I also thank my colleagues at Florida Atlantic University and elsewhere, as well as my students, who have helped me define my ideas through dialogue and debate. Heartfelt thanks also go to my former dean, Sandra K. Norton, and my department chair, Jan W. Hokenson, who have been constant sources of inspiration and support.

Without the love and encouragement of my friends and family, I would never have completed this project. Special thanks to my dear friends Nora Erro-Peralta, Julie Stephens, and Bonnie Lynne Smith. My deepest gratitude to my beloved Frank and to my patient, precious sons, Benjamin and Matthew. And always, to Leonard and Sally Robbins.

FRAMES
OF REFERENTS

Introduction:
The *Novísimos*, Postmodernism, and the Poetry of Guillermo Carnero

GUILLERMO Carnero's first book of poetry, *Dibujo de la muerte* [Sketch of death] appeared in 1967 during a period of transcontinental political upheaval from which Franco sought to shield his country. Indeed, in Spain at this time there were more limited expressions of the political movements that gained national appeal elsewhere in the West. Still, the Spanish *novísimo* poetry of the late 1960s and early 1970s was linked to another revolutionary movement of the day, the Western cultural rebellion that manifested itself in philosophy, in linguistics, and in artistic form. Its strategy was not to openly criticize the established order but to subvert it by calling into question the basis of all authority and by revealing the temporality of all ordering systems.

Many poets and critics of the *novísimo* period, especially those influenced by the generational paradigm, interpret this change in aesthetics as a break with the poetry written in Spain in the period immediately preceding the *novísimos*, and certainly there is no evidence of the explicitly social concerns and sentimentality of much poetry published in the 1940s and 1950s. Most critics acknowledge a link with the work of certain Spanish modernists, particularly those who focused on the problems of linguistic representation and produced antimimetic, meta-artistic texts.[1] However, there is clearly a relationship as well between this poetry and certain postwar aesthetic currents, represented in the 1940s and 1950s by poems published in *Postismo* and *Cántico*, and, in the 1950s and 1960s, by the poetry of Jaime Gil de Biedma, José Angel Valente, Claudio Rodríguez, and Carlos Bousoño.[2] Despite these echoes of prior aesthetic trends, the *novísimos* did not simply imitate those earlier poems; instead, they called into question the assumptions and claims of all artistic representation, in order to highlight the provisionality of representation itself. In fact, as I will explain shortly, their use of and allusion to modernist techniques and texts in conjunction with other images (pop culture, paintings, and texts from classical antiquity to the present) actually reveal a radical skepticism about language, art, meaning, and identity, which links *novísimo* poetry to certain expressions of postmodernism in other Western arts.[3]

The early works of the *novísimo* poets—Pere Gimferrer's *Arde el mar* (1966) [The sea is burning] and *Muerte en Beverly Hills* (1967) [Death in Beverly Hills], and Carnero's *Dibujo de la muerte* (1967)—were described by José María Castellet in his *Nueve novísimos poetas españoles* [Nine of the newest Spanish poets] as a break with the social and personal poetry of the 1950s and early 1960s. In his introduction to that anthology, Castellet offered a general definition of the group, while noting the stylistic differences between the individuals and especially between the older and the younger members of these poets—"los Seniors" (Manuel Vázquez Montalbán, Antonio Martínez Sarrión and José María Alvarez) and "la Coqueluche" (Félix de Azúa, Pedro Gimferrer, Vicente Molina-Foix, Guillermo Carnero, Ana María Moix and Leopoldo María Panero). In general, the characteristics he noted were these: a disregard for traditional forms; the use of certain vanguardist techniques, including automatic writing, elliptic techniques and collage; and the introduction of exotic elements and artfulness.[4] This definition has served as the starting point for all subsequent studies.

Later anthologies and criticism of the generation have placed less emphasis on "culturalismo," considered by Castellet to be a crucial defining characteristic of the generation. These works include in their definitions of the *novísimos* the innovations of several contemporary poets, such as José-Miguel Ullán, Jaime Siles, Jenaro Talens, Antonio Colinas, and Luis Antonio de Villena, who did not publish significant books of poetry until after Castellet's anthology appeared. They also take into account the move from culturalist aesthetics to metapoetry in the work of the poets Castellet discussed. Jaime Siles, for example, believes that the group should be named "la generación del lenguaje" [the language generation] for its preoccupation with the forms, language, and limits of poetic expression. He also notes the division of the generation into two stages, the first culturalist and the second metapoetic.[5] César Nicolás denies that there is a unifying aesthetic, but he calls the period from 1966 to 1977, "la nueva modernidad," the new modernity. He then notes the strength of the second, metapoetic stage of this poetry, in which

todo ello—y en particular el anterior culturalismo—se da como fragmentado
y pulverizado, como entrecortado o recorrido por una cierta angustia vital,
una nostalgia (Gimferrer), una trágica ironía (Carnero), o un discurso lúcido
y polimorfo (Panero) que, en los mejores ejemplos, inquietaba, interrumpía
y era máscara alucinante de una reflexión más profunda.

[all of it—and in particular the earlier culturalism—appears as fragmented
and pulverized, as broken or shot through with a certain vital anguish, a
nostalgia (Gimferrer), a tragic irony (Carnero), or a lucid and polymorphous
discourse (Panero) that, in the best examples, unsettled, interrupted, and was
the hallucinatory mask of a more profound reflection.]

He also discusses a third stage, from 1973 to 1977, in which the most distinguished poets became either silent or insane, and a fourth, from 1978 to 1988, which he believes to reflect a postmodern sensibility.[6]

Other critics have also challenged Castellet's definition of this generation. Víctor García de la Concha, for example, further disregards culturalism and explores the variety of *novísimo* poetics in his study "La renovación estética de los años sesenta" [The aesthetic renovation of the sixties].[7] José Olivio Jiménez also disputes the aesthetic coherence of the *novísimos*. He believes that this group should be called "the generation of 1970," because *novísimo* refers to one moment of the movement characterized by the use of

culturalismo, preciosismo o esteticismo verbal, neoirracionalismo, hermetismo
cifrado y personal, exploración—y hasta destrucción—del propio lenguaje,
reflexión metapoética en el verso, aprovechamiento (y esto fue lo más pasajero)
de la cultura de masas y la sensibilidad *camp*.[8]

[culturalism, preciosity or verbal aestheticism, neoirrationalism, encoded personal hermeticism, exploration—and even destruction—of language itself, metapoetic reflection in the verse, appropriation (and this was the most fleeting) of popular culture and camp sensibility.]

He asserts that there were actually several movements in the *novísimo* group:
(1) aestheticism (Carnero, Gimferrer, Colinas, Carvajal, Villena); (2) surrealism (Antonio Martínez Sarrión, Leopoldo María Panero); (3) culturalism (Gimferrer, Carnero, Villena, Colinas, Alvarez, Cuenca); (4) minimalism (Siles); (5) a personal critical hermeticism (Félix de Azúa, Marco Ricardo Barnatán); (6) linguistic experimentation (Talens, Ullán); (7) metapoetry (Carnero, Talens, Gimferrer, Azúa, Panero, Villena); (8) lyricism (Villena, the early Talens); and (9) postmodernism.[9]

Other critics have commented on the influence of earlier aesthetic movements in *novísimo* poetry. Víctor García de la Concha, for example, notes a certain baroque vision expressed in modernist style; for baroque poets, like the *novísimos*,

> se habían esforzado por llenar el vacío de desengaño y la desolación de la gran mentira con tipos e historias fingidas, retablos cargados de la mezcla más alucinada de mitos . . . en una plástica que, prolongando escultura en pintura, avasalla todos los recovecos del espacio.[10]

> [had strived to fill the vacuum of disillusionment and the desolation of the great lie with types and imaginary stories, scenes crowded with the most hallucinatory mixture of myths . . . in a visual space which, stretching sculpture into painting, transverses every pocket of space.]

The elliptic technique used by the *novísimos*, however, is more reminiscent of the modern, according to García de la Concha, because it becomes pure suggestion, allowing the reader to fill in the blanks.[11]

Detractors of the *novísimo* movement have consistently claimed that the poems were socially and politically inconsequential because they did not explicitly criticize the Franco regime and because they were inaccessible to the majority of readers.[12] The common reader could not understand *novísimo* poetry because the poems were highly intertextual, often alluding to texts and figures familiar only to a very select intellectual minority. Further difficulties arose from the metonymic, as opposed to metaphoric, nature of the poems: such texts do not readily communicate a message, political or otherwise, because, as I will explain, metonymic figures suggest a broad range of possible meanings, and they, therefore, cannot be as easily understood as a metaphor that "sums it all up" by embodying a meaning.[13]

Finally, *novísimo* poetry seemed irrelevant because it did not explain the poets' (or the Spaniards') social and political reality. In fact, it was often difficult to identify the referent of a *novísimo* poem, for the elliptic technique employed by so many of these poets, rather than highlighting and explaining reality or the referent (real or literary), served to elude and often eliminate it. For example, a *novísimo* poet who wished to develop ideas present in another poem would eliminate most of that poem's key elements, leaving only traces by which the reader might recognize the source, and would then re-place those traces in a new context.[14] This process was extremely frustrating to those critics who sought an easily identifiable meaning.[15]

The political and social relevance of these works further eluded critics because, even when the referent of a poem could be identified, it was much more likely to be a work of art, even the poem itself, than the injustice of the authoritarian regime. Thus, for example, while some critics consider the metapoetic phase to be a healthy period of self-criticism and reflection (Siles), others see in these changes either a form of conservatism (Talens) or a manifestation of an intellectual, rational, and creative crisis because they demonstrate "el sentimiento de la inutilidad de la literatura, de la poesía, la pérdida de fe en el valor activo de la palabra poética" [the feeling of the uselessness of literature, of poetry, the loss of faith in the active value of the poetic word].[16] As César Nicolás explains, "Se origina en realidad una fase de disolución y *crisis*: el poema, desvelado como ficción o *anatomía*, desenmascara su representación, acentúa su autoaniquilación, designa su mecanismo ilusorio: se hace abstracto y puramente autoreflexivo" [There really begins a phase of dissolution and *crisis*: the poem, revealed as fiction or *anatomy*, unmasks its representation, accents its self-annihilation, designates its illusory mechanism: it becomes abstract and purely self-reflective].[17] Here, the words "abstracto" and "puramente autoreflexivo" imply that the poetry is empty, and the word "autoaniquilación" suggests that it is no longer poetry at all. Rosa María Pereda further asserts that *novísimo* poetry reveals and comments upon its own irrelevance.[18] To many critics, metapoetry seemed to be merely an elaborate and socially irrelevant game wherein the poet revealed his or her own inadequacy. This criticism supports the erroneous belief that *novísimo* poetry is sterile because art that discusses artistic creation cannot simultaneously be about emotions, life, and society.

Castellet was one of the first Spanish critics to recognize the revolutionary content in *novísimo* poetry, which he likened to that of those European and American poets who ventured outside the traditionally poetic realm by incorporating elements of popular culture into their work and by disregarding poetic conventions. This chaotic and irreverent contemporary aesthetic was the reflection of a society whose values were no longer relevant and whose rules no longer held. In an authoritarian state, which by definition depends on a rigid system of rules and values, this aesthetic is particularly subversive. As Castellet notes, it transformed into icons those elements of society that were traditionally snubbed by the guardians of "culture."[19] However, as Castellet points out, the degree to which this phenomenon was a reaction purely to the circumstances of Spanish society is unclear, because the increased openness to foreign culture and aesthetics during the 1960s allows for the possibility that the Spaniards merely imitated trends that were successful elsewhere.[20] Fanny Rubio also feels that "El *crack* personal y privado que se observa en los hombres que escriben en otros países europeos en los últimos tiempos, está muy lejos de dejarse sentir en España" [The personal and private *crack* that may be observed in contemporary writers in other European countries is far from being felt in Spain].[21]

Luis Antonio de Villena suggests that these poets were aware of the revolutionary implications of their aesthetic foundations. He claims that even imitating foreign texts was a radical act aimed at subverting the authoritarian regime by rupturing the Franco-imposed cultural barriers.[22] The incorporation of foreign texts imbued with elements of the postmodern aesthetics represented a great threat to the political and social order established by the Franco regime, for the watchword of postmodernism is indeterminacy, and nothing could be more dangerous to a system grounded on the blind acceptance of the religious and political autocracy. Jaime Siles agrees that the language of the texts, the multiple allusions to film, the numerous quotations, and the general opacity of the texts had a political intent:

> Subvertía . . . el sistema de representación que es el lenguaje. Y, al subvertirlo (y por la forma de ese subvertirlo) transgredía el conjunto de las normas impuestas por aquél, descubriendo lo que éstas ocultan debajo: la falsedad de su disfraz.[23]

> [It subverted . . . the system of representation which is language. And, upon subverting it (and through the form of that subversion) it transgressed the group of norms imposed by it, uncovering what those norms were hiding: the falseness of its disguise.]

Another member of the *novísimo* generation, Pere Gimferrer, agrees that this poetry is subversive: "Toda poesía que no persiga la contravención expresa o tácita del sistema represivo de la sociedad, debe ser considerada como cómplice de este sistema" [All poetry that does not pursue the express or tacit countervention of the repressive social system should be considered an accomplice of that system].[24] Gimferrer certainly never believed that he, or other *novísimo* poets, supported Franco; their poetry, then, must undermine the Franco regime *tacitly*.

The revolutionary nature of these seemingly nonpolitical texts is also apparent to Carlos Bousoño. In his well-known introduction to *Ensayo de una teoría de la visión*, Guillermo Carnero's complete works to 1977, Bousoño describes the effect of neoaestheticism:

Las palabras nos remiten a un mundo que no es el de la experiencia, sino que el propio hecho poemático se ha encargado de construir. Dicho en forma distinta: el poema inventa su referente, del cual se constituye entonces un mero reflejo.[25]

[The words remit us to a world that is not that of experience, but rather that which the very poetic act has undertaken to construct. Said another way: the poem invents its referent, of which it then constitutes a mere reflection.]

And metapoetry has revolutionary implications:

toda crítica a la potencia deformadora de la realidad y la experiencia que posee el lenguaje en cuanto código dominado y manipulado por el Poder, *se convierte de suyo en una manifestación, no sólo de insolidaridad, sino de franca rebeldía contra ese Poder deshumanizador.*[26]

[any criticism of the potential to deform reality and experience that language possesses as a code dominated and manipulated by Power *becomes automatically a manifestation, not only of lack of solidarity, but of open rebellion against that dehumanizing Power.*]

This poetry, then, far from ignoring social reality, was intimately engaged in a dialogue with the language of power.

The analyses of these critics are astute and, I believe, accurate, but they do not fully describe the mechanisms by which this poetry subverts authority. If, as Andrew Debicki suggests in "Poesía española de la postmodernidad," Spanish poetry of the 1950s and 1960s is actually an early expression of postmodernism in Spain, some critics' blindness may be a result of their continuing to evaluate postwar poetry (1) in the context of Francoism, which leads them to expect an explicit criticism of social or political conditions; (2) in the context of Spanish literary history, which begs a rupture with the poets of the previous generation; and/or (3) in the context of modernist or pre-modernist aesthetics, which leads them to search for metaphor or symbol, resolution of paradox, formal innovation, and the communication of a set meaning.[27]

Given the number of lucid critiques of the generational concept in recent years,[28] it may be fruitful at this juncture to depart from the Spanish literary context in order to consider the relationship between *novísimo* poetry and Western postmodern aesthetics, with which the *novísimos* were familiar, despite the cultural barriers erected by Francoism (Carnero, for example, read Heidegger, Barthes, and Foucault and subscribed to *Tel Quel*).[29] Postmodern poetry departs from a different philosophical position than modernism; it is derived in part from a post-Saussurean recognition of the arbitrary relationship between signified and signifier, an insight that has ramifications not only for the poetic representation of reality but also for "reality" itself, which comes to be seen as a social construction rather than a reflection of some eternal, transcendental realm. Postmodern works call attention to this constructivism in part through the manipulation and foregrounding of various framing mechanisms, such as intertextuality, metadiscourse, and literary form, which imply that reality, as well as art, is framed by interpretive conventions.[30]

Postmodern poetry also represents the ways in which chance connections often constitute a meaning that, although necessarily temporal and temporary, may seem absolute. It does so by foregrounding repetition, metonymy, and intertextuality; resisting structural closure; rejecting traditional forms or using them arbitrarily; recognizing only poetic reality; questioning canonic assumptions; and highlighting the limitations of language. These characteristics are apparent in the *novísimo* techniques mentioned above—the reference only to artistic reality, the predominance of metonymy over metaphor, the lack of structure or the random use of it, the use of irrational or hermetic images or constructions, and the reference to, use of, and parody of the style and imagery of earlier poetry.

Despite the highly intellectual and abstract nature of this critique of reality, postmodern poetry is vitally engaged with the fundamental problems of human existence and understanding. Its foregrounding of the fictitious nature of art highlights the artificiality of human structures and reveals the unresolved paradoxes of life—the expressiveness and inadequacy of language, the instability of balanced structures (such as poems), and the interplay of power and subjection (as between poet and readers). Thus, although these poems seem to treat only poetic judgment, poetic uncertainty, and poetic authority, they have broader implications because the poet, the poem, and language are part of a community. As Carnero himself said in an interview with José Luis Jover, poetic discourse may be taken as a synecdochical representation of society because language is not an entity apart from society but, rather, a representative element of society, one that reflects the conflicts and conditions of the world in which it is situated.[31] The revelation of the inherent instability of language, for example, implies that the meaning of even the most dogmatic political or religious statement is ambiguous.

The rejection by *novísimo* poets of metaphor also has profound political implications. Poststructuralist critics deny the New Critical claim that meaning can ever be "embodied," "captured," or "reflected" in a metaphor, because individual words do not exist in a vacuum but in linguistic, historical, social, political, cultural, and literary contexts, and they therefore inevitably suggest diverse meanings to the various readers of a text. Thus, even so simple an image as "her hair was gold" suggests a plurality of possible interpretations. For example, one could explore the relationship between men and women implicit in the image, social attitudes concerning wealth, and the concept of beauty both in the context in which the image was produced and in that in which it is currently being read and interpreted. This plurality of the metaphoric image suggested to Paul de Man that "Metaphor is error because it believes or feigns to believe in its own referential meaning. The belief is legitimate only within the limits of a given text."[32] Umberto Eco has even claimed that all language is based on metonymy, since the two elements of a metaphor must have some contiguous connection for the image to work.[33] It follows for postmodernists that metonymy provides a more accurate representation of the world's complexity because it seeks to show some of the connections among words and images, words and world.[34] According to Joseph Conte, it is for this reason that metonymy is the predominant trope of one kind of postmodern poetic form, which he denominates the "series," because metonymy effectively represents the random nature of the connections between "a set of tangencies."[35]

The foregrounding of intertextuality also invites us to rethink the value and values of once-stable regimes by demonstrating that their beliefs did not represent absolute, universal truths but culturally determined perspectives. For example, the poetic representation of a historical figure forces us to reconsider the previously unquestioned truth of that history and of the values it sought to perpetuate, because we see that the figure in the historical text must also be fictitious, equally determined by the prejudices of the author, the reader, and their contexts. What is more, the fact that the figure or event appears now in a new historical and literary context reminds us that its original context has disappeared and highlights the fact that the vision of any culture is limited and temporary. Similarly, the allusion to other literary and artistic works unmasks the dependence of artistic discourse upon the historical legacy of aesthetic theory and practice.

This seeming "much ado about nothing" has important implications, for some contemporary critics see a grave danger in the assumption that metaphors can magically embody meaning. Geoffrey Hartman sees in the "pure" image, or the quest for that image, the basis for authoritarianism, since the goal of any authoritarian system is the creation and use of a language whose meaning will seem to be so obvious as to be unquestionable.[36] He prefers language with multiple referentiality and unresolved tensions, for the "richer or more loaded language is by quotation or allusion, the more it can subvert meaning."[37] Thus, allusive and metonymical language is most subversive, for its textuality serves as "an antibody to body-images of power and presence."[38] The reliance by *novísimo* poets on such language is, in this sense, a political statement, for it undermines the apparently stable and irrefutable equivalences established by authority.

Other techniques, such as the destabilization of poetic structure, undermine the seeming immortality of authoritarian regimes by suggesting that orderly systems contain the seeds of their own destruction. Early *novísimo* poetry breaks with authoritarian structures by rejecting the exalted conventions of the Spanish lyric, opting instead for a self-generating verse. Carnero's early poems, for example, correspond to Joseph Conte's definition of the postmodern serial form: the form is determined in an aleatory manner, that is, through the random metonymic connections between words, figures, and images.[39] The serial form reflects a radical change in the concepts of language, poetic form, and the image: in the view of postmodernists, there is no inherent or essential correspondence between these techniques and meaning; and meaning itself is seen as plurivalent and contingent. The structure of Carnero's early poetry thus represents a dual rebellion against Francoism: traditional forms are repudiated, and authoritarian meaning is placed into doubt.

However, even the use of traditional poetic form—like Carnero's use of the sonnet in his latest work—may subvert the concept of poetic order in postmodern poetry; it is simply another means of exploring the implications of ordering systems. This use of form is perfectly consonant with a postmodern poetics, since, as Brian McHale explains, the foregrounding of meter and rhyme is an effective strategy for highlighting ontological questions and for underscoring the chaos of the world.

> Arbitrariness is foregrounded—arbitrariness, that is, at the level of world; at the level of word, there is no arbitrariness at all, the shape of the text being predetermined by the fixed order....[40]

Joseph Conte also explains how the use of traditional forms in postmodern poetry highlights the artificiality of order, and he argues as well for the sociopolitical significance of these formal changes, which constituted a response to the deference to form in the United States of the 1950s.[41] The situation in Spanish poetry was very similar; in fact, the *Garcilaso* sonnets were even more explicitly linked to conservative politics than their American counterparts.[42] The American poets of the 1960s responded to this poetic conservatism by using procedural, or structured, forms to highlight the "ontological illogic" beneath the surface of seemingly perfect structures.[43] Far from mirroring or proposing an orderly world, then, the traditional forms of Carnero's later poetry provide a critique of ordering systems through the revelation of their artificiality and limitations.[44]

Other poetic devices serve to explore the question of power in any system. For example, metapoetry, and specifically the technique of placing an unreliable or self-contradictory speaker in the text, undermines the absolute power of authority, because it reveals the cracks in the mask of power,[45] and it thus allows us to question "the very bases of any . . . standards of judgment. Who sets them? When? Where? Why?"[46] Furthermore, the unresolved paradoxes in *novísimo* poetry undermine the good/bad dichotomy of social poetry by suggesting that seeming opposites are interdependent.[47] This indeterminacy in *novísimo* poetry unsettled the modern vision of a stable, knowable world.

Even the focus on the disintegration of the coherent self may have political significance, especially in Carnero's poetry, where that self is explicitly and implicitly linked to images, texts, and forms. The individual may be seen as a microcosm of society, constituted as well by the random intertextuality of signifying systems. As Paul Bové explains:

> As power disperses itself, it opens up specific fields of possibility; it constitutes entire domains of action, knowledge, and social being by shaping the institutions and disciplines in which, for the most part, we largely make ourselves. In these domains we become the individuals, the subjects, that they make us. . . . [T]he subject comes to be whatever or whoever he or she is only *within* this set of discursive and nondiscursive fields. "Individuation" then is the space in which we are most regulated by the ruling disciplines of language, sexuality, economics, culture, and psychology.[48]

The recognition of the plurality of the self undermines authority by destabilizing the image of the authoritarian figure; thus Julia Kristeva asserts that this shift in focus from an accepted homogeneous structure to the plurality of the speaker will undermine the authority of accepted systems of thought.[49]

Finally, *novísimo* poetry subverts power by ignoring it: by simultaneously accepting and subverting the myriad systems of discourse that have unsuccessfully attempted to explain reality, it undermines the legitimacy of authorities that seek to impose a single truth on a population. Indeed, despite criticism charging these poets with frivolity and irrelevant culturalism, their poetry may be more subversive than the previous generations' explicitly social poetry written for the immense majority. The *novísimos* might argue that the latter actually supported the Franco regime by recognizing, and thus consolidating, its power.[50] First, the ineffective criticism of the social poets actually made the regime seem more powerful by making all protest appear futile. Furthermore, those verbal attacks may have created support for the government by making it appear to be the victim of "unfair" criticism. The *novísimos*, in contrast, refused to play into the hands of the Franco regime by discussing its oppression explicitly. Rather, they undermined authority's power by ignoring it and by questioning the basis for all knowledge and language, including that which the government presented as irrefutable. The absence of Francoism extended even to the poetics preferred by the *novísimo* generation: they consciously avoided the neoclassical structures of the *Garcilaso* poets, along with the neoromantic sentimentality of their detractors, in favor of forms of popular culture or the more intellectual, surrealist, and abstract poetry of the writers associated with *Cántico* and *Postismo*.[51]

In sum, the linguistic play in *novísimo* poetry has a serious import, since it challenges the boundaries of discourse, representation and meaning, and it thereby surreptitiously undermines the dominant authority. As Jean-François Lyotard explains,

> Reactional countermoves are no more than programmed effects in the opponent's strategy; they play into his hands and thus have no effect on the balance of power. That is why it is important to increase displacement in the games, and even to disorient it, in such a way as to make an unexpected "move" (a new statement).[52]

It is clear, then, that the preoccupation with representation need not imply an evasion of social concerns. Rather, by foregrounding the inadequacy of language, literature can call into question the authority of any absolute system of meaning.[53] It is, in this sense, an exploration and a critique of the consequences of what Lyotard deems the metanarratives of modernity, including the Enlightenment, Marxism, capitalism and positivism.[54] The criticism of structures is simply not limited to the social or the political, nor is there any faith in a better alternative, or "progress."

This skepticism toward the "metanarratives characteristic of modernity," which seek to "legitimize knowledge in terms not of the past but of the future" could lead to nihilism.[55] I would argue, however, that the *novísimos*, and specifically Carnero, could better be described as "liberal ironists," to use Richard Rorty's term; that is, they are liberals who recognize the contingency of their beliefs.[56] Rorty also explains how the ideas of these liberal ironists have been misinterpreted as conservatism by "nonintellectuals," who still believe in an essentialist kind of order, but he claims that "Hostility to a particular historically conditioned and possibly transient form of solidarity is not hostility to solidarity as such."[57]

The inevitable demise of every culture, every regime, every interpretation, is a constant concern in Carnero's poetry. His poems reveal that knowledge is both generated and limited by its contexts and that those contexts are themselves temporal and partial. One way in which they do so is through the allusion to a variety of historical periods and aesthetic visions. Thus, despite his denomination by some critics as a neosymbolist, neobaroque, or neopositivist poet, Carnero does not merely transplant works from different periods; rather he juxtaposes them in order to foreground the historical instability of such concepts as "unity," "meaning," "order," and "presence."[58] For example, the appearance of baroque, neoclassical, modernist, and symbolist techniques or figures recontextualizes them and places them in dialogue with one another. The competing views of meaning, order, and identity of those periods are placed on the same plane, encouraging the reader to recognize and contemplate the assumptions underlying "transparent" notions of poetic or personal meaning as well as their temporality. Thus, by revealing the plurality and contingency of aesthetic values, allusion serves to destabilize frozen concepts of meaning, identity, and language. This subversion is not explicitly political, for it is not aimed at any specific regime, nor does it value one type of government over another, but it does have political import because it posits the eventual obliteration of every system of order, which will be shattered, dispersed, and eliminated by the elements of the infinite universe that it was unable to integrate in its vision.

Metonymy functions in a similar way: the repeated recontextualization of metaphors reveals that their meaning is based on chance contiguities and constituted through time and repetition. This process expands and fragments meaning, exploding the apparent unity and atemporality of metaphor.[59]

The metonymic expansion of imagery thus mirrors Carnero's use of allusion, because it historicizes that which is apparently eternal and challenges the notion that meaning can ever be finally arrested in language.

Especially in *Dibujo de la muerte* (1967), intertextuality and metonymy undermine hegemonic interpretations of reality and personal identity by suggesting the importance of chance in the constitution of meaning. In *Dibujo de la muerte*, this concept is tied to the problem of personal identity through a speaker who is reflected in artists or works of art from a previous age and thus tied to their temporality and fragmentation. I have chosen to focus on this fragmented self in my analysis of *Dibujo de la muerte* in chapter 1, in part because I believe that by doing so, I may counter the accusation of impersonality that has been leveled at this particular instance of culturalist poetry. The allusions in *Dibujo de la muerte* are numerous and diverse, but they are not purely ornamental; rather they are linked to the emotional crisis of the speaker, who sees his own hopelessly fragmented identity in their limitations. The poetry in the book is difficult, but, far from eluding emotion, it represents a profound sense of despair.

In *El sueño de Escipión* (1971) [Scipio's dream], this emotion is expressed in the speaker's self-critical metapoetic musings, which are linked to a plurality of Western writers through quotations and scholarly footnotes. Rather than supporting his arguments, these critical citations foreground the disagreement between Western authors and scholars regarding the meaning and form of art and reality. The book thereby suggests that meaning is not "discovered" but derived from a history of discourse (in this case, Western philosophy and aesthetic theory) and subject to revision or refutation. Chapter 2 studies the ways in which this use of metapoetry and scholarly discourse undermines the power of author-ity by revealing its provisionality (in the unsettled debates), along with the conflicts and motivations of the author and his financial and artistic dependence upon a cooperative reading public. These concerns are not limited to literary issues, but clearly outline the general mechanism of power, including political power: it is contingent, temporal, and dependent upon the cooperation of divergent subjects.

Chapter 3 focuses on *Variaciones y figuras sobre un tema de La Bruyère* (1974) [Variations and figures on a theme by La Bruyère], a book that also suggests that meaning is not intrinsic but a function of repetition; the book paradoxically uses repetition to reincorporate time and history into its own fixed structure. The title of the book indicates one form of repetition that appears in Carnero's book, that is, semantic repetition, since all of the poems are variations or figures on the same theme; however, lexical repetition and formal repetition are also featured. The theme is the stultification of language, form, and meaning; the repetitions both represent and unravel those hardened structures. This concept is not new to Carnero—both metonymy and allusion are forms of repetition—but *Variaciones y figuras* foregrounds poetic form and suggests that time may loosen even that rigid and apparently static structure.

El azar objetivo (1975) [Objective chance], which I study in conjunction with one of Carnero's critical essays in chapter 4, aims squarely at the fragile lens of rationality, which it attempts to rupture with fragments of the irrational. The structure and language of the book parody the rational forms of the critical essay, the premises of which are explicitly criticized in the poems. Several inexplicable images and allusions, and a generous dose of grim humor, also suggest that, although the forms of rationality may appear logical, rationality itself is ontologically illogical. Its illusion of order is safe and comforting but sterile and fundamentally limited, unstable, and circular. It does not allow for chance or mystery, and either of these could easily destroy its neat paradigms and principles.

In *Divisibilidad indefinida* (1990) [Indefinite divisibility] Carnero looks retrospectively at his own work, at Western concepts of the self and artistic form, and at the tradition of retrospective literature itself; I do the same in chapter 5. This book alludes to *Dibujo de la muerte* in its lyricism and neoclassical images; to *El sueño de Escipión* in the foregrounding of an ironic speaker; to *Variaciones y figuras* in the forms of repetition; and to *El azar objetivo* in the critique of rationality. References to the *Libro de Alexandre*, Garcilaso de la Vega, neoclassical concepts of order, romantic lyricism, Rubén Darío, T. S. Eliot, Juan Ramón Jiménez, and Jorge Guillén suggest that the scope of this retrospection extends beyond Carnero's own work. These allusions in fact contextualize Carnero's work within the history of the Western lyric. As in *Dibujo*, the linguistic, imagic, and philosophical fragmentation that the speaker of *Divisibilidad indefinida* observes and analyzes has profound repercussions for his own identity, which likewise becomes shattered and dispersed. The conclusion to *Divisibilidad indefinida* is considerably more optimistic than Carnero's previous work, suggesting a possible healing of the infinitely divided self, language, vision; however, the irony with which the speaker describes prior attempts at unity undermines to some extent this final comforting image.

The interpretive frames that I use to study each of Guillermo Carnero's books are in some sense arbitrarily imposed upon them, but they are consistent with the philosophical bases of the poetry. Thus the lens through which I analyze *Dibujo de la muerte*—the implications for the poet and the reader of intertextual and contextual fragmentation—could be trained on the other books as well. The critique of the author is important throughout Carnero's work, though I only concentrate on it in my study of *El sueño de Escipión*; and, as I have explained, repetition is an essential technique in every book, not just *Variaciones y figuras*. *El azar objetivo* targets the critical essay, but rationality is a constant mark of Carnero's poetry, and all of it, not just *Divisibilidad indefinida*, is retrospective. I recognize the temporal and interpretive limits of these frames, as Carnero does in his poetry, and I encourage other readers to shift them and substitute others, to continue to melt even my frozen frames.

1
Framing the Self in
Dibujo de la muerte

GUILLERMO Carnero's first book, *Dibujo de la muerte*, appeared in 1967 and seemed to be the perfect target for critics opposed to *novísimo* elitism. The poems of this book are highly intertextual, often alluding to and borrowing from the voices of artists and personalities from distant lands and epochs: Paul Scarron, Brummel, Watteau, Oscar Wilde, Ludovico Manin, Juan Sforza, and Iacopo Guarana all write, fret, paint, and compose their way through these poems of "analogous historical personages."[1] In none of the book's twenty-six poems is there any mention of Franco, of the civil war, of "la inmensa mayoría," the vast majority of Spanish social poetry. In fact, Spain only appears once, and it is not contemporary Spain we see but the fictitious Castille created by Cervantes's imagination and recreated by Carnero's. This poetry is clearly not addressed to the common reader; it is not even addressed to the common intellectual, since most critics must spend as much time studying Carnero's sources as his creations. In Carnero's first book, it seems that poetry is not the voice of the people but a puzzle whose pieces will never form a coherent picture of reality and whose social relevance must therefore be questioned.

No one has denied that it is a beautiful and complicated puzzle: the poetry in this book is a breathtaking display of imagic and intellectual complexity. Even the title—*Dibujo de la muerte*—suggests the plurality of meanings and the complexity of expression that its texts contain. In the words "sketch of death" we see the interrelation of death and art and that of the plastic arts (sketch) and literature (the sketch is composed of words). Its incomplete form—it is not a full rendering, but a sketch—suggests the futility of the artistic endeavor, for the artist can only hope to represent a trace of meaning. This futility is also suggested by the image of death, which represents not only *the* end, the end of our lives and our culture, but also *an* end—the final resting place of knowledge. And, as we will see in Carnero's subsequent books, every pursuit of knowledge leads to this dead end and leaves behind only the traces of the quest.

The social and political implications of the philosophy underlying *Dibujo de la muerte* are not immediately apparent, especially to readers accustomed to traditional forms of literary expression such as realism, symbolism, or modernism, which seek to represent a mimetic reality or a transcendent ideal. The poems of *Dibujo de la muerte* do not attempt to represent an essential meaning or reality but rather the impossibility of representation, "the unpresentable in presentation itself," by shifting the reader's focus from *reality* or *meaning* to the limits of their representation, since "the limits are themselves the stakes," including the limits between texts, between text and reader, between text and writer, and between writer and reader.[2] These limits are tested in *Dibujo de la muerte* by the interplay of metonymic images, intertextuality, meta-artistic discourse and negation, which link these poems to one another, to the Western literary and artistic tradition that frames them, and to the reality, including the personal reality of emotions, that art has sought to represent or frame. These techniques suggest that we can never fully know or represent "reality": we are always left only with a web of discourse weaving itself incessantly around an impenetrable void. This web is the skeleton we leave behind when we and our culture pass; thus, the re-presentation of this tradition of partial interpretations of the world, this heap of frames, is indeed a sketch of death.

Both the imagery and the allusions in *Dibujo de la muerte* suggest the multiplicity and contingency of what we call "reality." The metonymic connections reveal how reality is constituted and reconstituted by chance, rather than necessary, encounters. Here these random meetings come to constitute the form of the poems, which may be described as serial—in Conte's terms, "a poetic form in which the syntagmatic relation of the sign is predominant."[3] This approach to poetic creation differs markedly from the use of structured poetic form and metaphor as means to embody essences.

Intertextuality also suggests the plurivalence and instability of meaning. In its broadest sense, it refers to the trace of all prior texts and contexts in every enunciation, as Julia Kristeva explains:

> The term *intertextuality* denotes this transposition of one (or several) sign-system(s) into another.... If one grants that every signifying practice is a field of transpositions of various signifying systems (an intertextuality), one then

1 / Framing the Self in *Dibujo de la muerte* 31

understands that its "place" of enunciation and its denoted "object" are never single, complete and identical to themselves, but always plural, shattered, capable of being tabulated. In this way polysemy can also be seen as the result of a semiotic polyvalence—an adherence to different sign-systems.[4]

The complex and multiple allusions in *Dibujo de la muerte* suggest this definition of intertextuality and thus represent synecdochically the inherent multiplicity of every artistic creation as well as its circumscription by its artistic, social, and linguistic contexts.[5]

This particular interpretation of the world is presented in *Dibujo de la muerte* by several speakers, who appear to be detached from the social reality they observe, but who are shown to be framed by that reality even as they create their own artistic frames for it. These speakers are either artists (Watteau, Oscar Wilde, Brummel), artistic creations (Don Quijote), or artistic creations who are also artists (Aschenbach from *Death in Venice*). They all recognize the meaninglessness of human existence and seek to transcend it through art, but they find that art is inextricably tied to the human realm by its tools, be they language, paint, clay, musical instruments, or costumes. Thus, when the artist seeks to penetrate the mystery, to reach the place "beneath the water" ("Muerte en Venecia") or behind the glitter of the material world ("Les charmes de la vie"), he finds only his own fragmented face reflected on the surface.[6] And, of course, all of these artists are framed as well by the poems in which they appear, which alter their literary and artistic identities.

The technique of placing artists within a work of art reveals a central concern that recurs throughout Carnero's poetry: artists are ultimately reflections of their contexts, and, despite their recognition of the limits of their cultures, they must work within them and inevitably die with them, leaving only their works, their sketches of death. This recognition extends beyond the personae of the poems because these artistic speakers are often identified through their interpretive activities with "the reader" and through their creative and critical activities with the artistic and scholarly personae of "Guillermo Carnero."[7] The transgression of textual boundaries, then, has philosophical implications because it extends the notion of the constructed self beyond the limits of the text and beyond purely artistic concerns.[8]

The interconnection of texts and contexts, and the simultaneous representation and subversion of meaning, identity, and authority, begin in "Ávila," the very first poem of *Dibujo de la muerte*. This poem introduces some of the most important figures of the book—silence, death, emptiness, art, words—and its principal techniques: metonymy, description of a past artistic work, and an artistic speaker. In "Avila," a modern speaker contemplates and linguistically recreates the stone statues of the medieval city in the first part of the poem, and he discusses their inability to transcend their cultural and temporal contexts in the second part. Readers are lead to a parallel experience through the form of the poem and through its imagery, which interweaves life, art, and death. The surprising contrasts—the words wrenched from their accustomed contexts and placed metonymically in contact with other, seemingly contradictory, words and contexts—reveal the instability and ultimate mortality of words, ideas, and dreams. The poem thus allows us to feel the emptiness that cultural forms acquire over time, the limitations of every vision of the world.

The contingency of reality and its representations is presented structurally in "Avila" through the jarring juxtaposition of images of life, death, and art. This process creates sequential palinodes, or affirmations followed by negations, requiring that readers repeatedly reverse their expectations.[9] Thus, at the beginning of the poem, the statues seem to be dead, since "de los cuellos tronchados sólo brota el mismo mármol que se entrelaza al borde de los dedos / en un contenido despliegue de pétalos y ramas" [from the split necks only the same marble springs, which intertwines on the brink of the fingers / in a restrained unfolding of petals and branches].[10] The following images, however, suggest that there is life, or the possibility or hope of it, within the dead forms:

> la morbidez, las redondas mejillas de los niños nacidos al mármol para
>   la muerte,
> los senos vagamente estériles de las Parcas diluidas en rígidos ramos de
>   volutas y frutos,
> el doloroso latir de las irisadas tibias sobre los cojincillos de mármol
>   ondulados
> como para ofrecer un reposo caliente y amortiguar la delgadez helada
> de esa mano de ámbar que acaricia con el pausado ritmo de la lluvia
> la cabeza de un perro también muerto en la piedra.
>
> [morbidity, the round cheeks of the children born into marble for death
> the vaguely sterile breasts of the Parcae dissolved in rigid clusters of
>   volutes and fruits,
> the painful beating of the tepid iridescence on the marble cushions,
>   undulating

1 / Framing the Self in *Dibujo de la muerte*

as if to offer a warm repose and deaden the frigid slenderness
of that amber hand that caresses with the deliberate rhythm of the rain
the head of a dog also dead in the stone.]

The contiguity of words suggesting life, death, reality, and art creates uncertainty: where we expect to find life, as in "las redondas mejillas de los niños nacidos," we only find art, which converts life into stone, "nacidos al mármol para la muerte," and where we then expect lifeless art, we find warmth, "el doloroso latir," "un reposo caliente." This technique repeatedly frustrates the readers' expectations, reproducing poetically the unresolved ambiguity the speaker perceives in the stone. The confluence of life, death, and art in the first part of "Ávila," then, reminds us that the representation of reality is not identical to reality itself; it is an interpretation, a selection of often-contradictory details that do not resolve the complexity of the world.

In the second part of the poem, the speaker discusses the problem of art, and specifically of the work of art described and reproduced in the first part of the poem. He suggests that the mortality of the objects represented in the sculpture is compounded by the mortality of the sculpture itself, for the artist who hoped to communicate something transcendent and eternal through it developed his vision in a cultural context, and both artist and culture are long dead. The imagery of this section demonstrates the tension between the past, represented by the work of art, and the present. It reveals that this work of art is silent specifically to us, that there exists an unbridgeable gap between the remains of antiquity and the modern world. For that reason,

> A pesar de la noche, es imposible reconstruir su muerte.
> Ir ensamblando antiguos inciensos y sudarios,
> medallones, y viene hasta mí el golpeteo
> de un caballo en los lisos espejos de la noche,
> es imposible, nadie sabrá, ni esas raíces
> ni esas pequeñas uvas de humedad y salitre
> ni ese tenue azabache como el salto de un pájaro
> que al trasluz se desliza en los atardeceres
> al fondo de la carne de los ángeles muertos en el mármol.
>
> (78)

[In spite of the night, it is impossible to reconstruct its death.
To go about assembling ancient incenses and shrouds,

medallions, and to have come toward me the hammering
of a horse on the smooth mirrors of the night,
it is impossible, no one will know, not those roots
nor the small grapes of moisture and saltpeter
nor that tenuous jet like the bound of a bird
which glides against the light of the afternoons
at the heart of the flesh of the angels dead in the marble.]

These images suggest that the work can no longer speak to us, we cannot understand it, because we live in a different culture, and that other culture in which it was constructed is irremediably gone. This conflict is presented through the contiguity of images from ancient and modern times: "inciensos y sudarios" and an "azabache" can only coexist in the modern world, and this very coexistence limits our understanding of a culture that only included the former images and that is separated from us by "el sordo sonido de los siglos" [the deaf sound of the centuries]. Despite their aspirations to heaven or even to life, works of art cannot represent the same vision forever because they are partial, and they remain tied by their form and their style to the human realm, to their creator, and to the context in which they were created. For this reason, the speaker concludes that we cannot entertain the slightest hope for immortality in art:

> Por eso, entre el inmenso latido de la noche,
> elevado entre un rumor de vides húmedas, es triste
> no tener siquiera un puñado de palabras, un débil
> recuerdo tibio, para aquí, en la noche,
> imaginar que algún día podremos
> inventarnos, que al fin hemos vivido.

(79)

> [For that reason, in the immense beating of the night,
> elevated amidst the rumor of humid grapevines, it is sad
> not to have even a handful of words, a feeble
> tepid memory, here, in the night, to
> imagine that one day we will be able
> to invent ourselves, that at last we have lived.]

The speaker feels intensely the tension between the immortality of the world and the mortality of human beings and all their creations, the impossibility of transcendence inherent in the image. The images of this poem, then, do not represent a symbolic or eternal meaning, but, rather, the limitations of artistic representation.

The foregrounding of meta-artistic concerns invites us to contemplate the structure and temporality of this particular poem and of its creator. In the first part of the poem, the contiguity of life, death, and art in the description of the sculpture creates a tension between a seemingly atemporal artistic form and the necessarily temporal condition of human existence. In the second part, these tensions and limitations are extended to a specific human being, the speaker, who is apparently an interpreter of the work of art described in the first part and a creator of others—"También tú has recibido la oscura herencia de un inmenso dominio inaccesible / que no tiene ni principio ni fin ni esperanza en el tiempo" [You too have received the obscure inheritance of an immense, inaccessible domain / that has not beginning nor end nor hope in time]. The word "también" suggests an identification between the speaker and the creator of the sculpture. This dual position as creator and interpreter parallels that of "the poet," the implied creator of this poem, and "Guillermo Carnero," who is both literary critic and poet, and who thereby may be identified in part with the speaker and thus framed by the work he creates. There are also implications for the reality of "the reader" of the poem, who could be interpreted as the "tú" of the second part of "Ávila," and who may also be identified with the speaker of these lines, the "reader" of the sculpted figures of Ávila. This framing technique extends the implications of the illusory immortality of art into the worlds of the poet and the reader and suggests that even the self is a work of art, a temporal construction.[11]

The same images of death and the same techniques—metonymy, allusion to prior artistic works, and a prominent speaker—predominate in "Muerte en Venecia," a poem that also expresses the disintegration of a coherent self and the sense of loss created by the failed search for unity and a transcendent ideal. This extremely complex poem weaves together imagery, texts, and personae in order to show the limits of representation and human understanding. This technique compels the reader to make connections among images and among several literary works, to become involved in the creative process and in the work of art itself, and thereby to experience the impenetrable complexity of the world and the partiality of any representation of it.[12]

The reader is initially tempted to abandon this complexity by a speaker who, in the first part of the poem, appears to have transcended reality and who beckons him, and Detlev Spinell, "beyond words," to the other side of the water, a place where meaning resides and contradictions are resolved. Several allusions to works by Thomas Mann suggest, however, that there is no such place, that in the world contradictory elements inevitably coexist. The same is suggested by the repeated negation of a deep meaning below the surface of things by the speaker in the second part of the poem. The imagery also implies that meaning is plurivalent and ultimately incomprehensible. It is impossible to reduce any of the figures of this poem to a single meaning: like the images of "Avila," they evoke several contradictory meanings at once. These techniques, then, undermine the speaker's seductive claims by revealing the impossibility of his incredible dream of transcendence and resolution.

The speaker's beckoning of Detlev Spinell begins in the first lines of the poem, as does the development of enigmatic and often contradictory imagery. The speaker seems to speak to Spinell from another realm, to tell him, "Detlev Spinell, son aquí debajo / de la muerte" (86) [Detlev Spinell, they are here (the sound here) beneath / death]. The complication of meaning through language begins with the word, "son," which points the reader in two different directions: is it a noun or a verb? If it is a verb, who are "they," the subject of the verb? The next phrase, "debajo de la muerte," may lead us to conclude that "son" is the noun "sound," because we would expect the verb "están" (unless the subject of the verb is an event or permanent); however, we are then left without a verb. Is "son" then meant as a metonymic representation or suggestion of Detlev Spinell, the musician who is the protagonist of Mann's *Tristan?* Our expectations are further frustrated by the mixture of the concrete and the abstract: "debajo" sets up the expectation of something physical (and "Venecia" implies it will be water), but instead we get the abstract "muerte," death. This short stanza establishes the pattern of ambiguity and frustrated expectations that we will see throughout the poem.

The process of substitution and expansion of images continues in the next stanza. The water of Venice is replaced by a variety of images, both from Mann's novella and from Carnero's work:

> La sangre de la noche
> por el parque, las alas de la noche
> por el agua del parque, hasta la sangre
> los ojos submarinos, las palomas
> el negro viento de su pelo, el agua
> por el kiosko, por las porcelanas

1 / Framing the Self in *Dibujo de la muerte* 37

azules, por los álamos, la orilla
de la noche, los mimbres destejidos
de la noche.

[The blood of the night
through the park, the wings of the night
through the water of the park, up to the blood
the submarine eyes, the pigeons
the black wind of his hair, the water
through the kiosk, through the porcelains
of blue, through the poplars, the shore
of the night, the unwoven twigs
of the night.]

The explanation of this series of images is complicated, because none can stand on its own; the impact of this stanza is created by the confluence of imagic patterns. The images are related and finally substituted for one another solely on the basis of their contiguity. They may be equated on a grammatical basis—for example, "sangre," "alas," "orilla," and "mimbres destejidos" are related because, in the sentence, they are all "de la noche," of the night. Images may also be related by their location: we know that something is beneath both death and water ("ojos submarinos," "debajo / de la muerte"). They may be related through another image—water flows through "el kiosko," "las porcelanas," and "los álamos"—or by their own actions: water and blood flow identically. Images are also equated by their physical proximity in a verse. Thus, in the lines "hasta la sangre / los ojos submarinos, las palomas / el negro viento de su pelo, el agua" a connection is made between the doves and the eyes, implying that they are both submerged (in water or blood?), and among the wind, the night, the water, and someone's hair. Further metonymic connections are made among images based on the characteristics of those images: birds fly in the wind and are therefore like hair blowing in the wind; the hair becomes black wind for its movement in the wind of the night. As we read, we continue to see interconnections. The trees are associated with the hair because they are blown by the wind and thus can be called "destejidos" [unbraided] and with the birds because they are also blowing in the night wind. The black and white are also reminiscent of piano keys, and of ink and paper, thereby suggesting a link between artistic creation, transcendence, and death. The plurivalence of these images is further expanded by their metonymic connection with the imagery of *Death in Venice*, with its bloodred strawberries, flowing water, and, of course, death. We are left to wonder where those "ojos submarinos" are—under death, under water, or under blood—not to mention *what* they are (the mystery or its explanation? the subject of the first sentence, if "son" is a verb being substituted for "están," perhaps to suggest permanence?). By the time we reach the end of the stanza, the images are so interwoven that they can no longer be separated. They, like the world they seek to represent, cannot be reduced to a simple correspondence.

The imagery and the concepts become even more complicated in the following stanza, in which transcendence is implicitly linked to death.

> Debajo de su nombre,
> del borroso marchamo, demasiada
> fue su belleza por entre las barbas
> de sus antepasados, los blasones
> y el yeso colorado de los culos
> de los ángeles.

> [Beneath his name,
> the blurred stamp, too great
> was his beauty for among the beards
> of his forefathers, the coats of arms
> and the florid plaster of the asses
> of angels.]

Structurally, "nombre" is now related to "muerte," which is related to water ("*sub*marinos"), which is related to night and blood and all we have above. It is also related to the sign ("borroso marchamo"), the origin of meaning, which is repeatedly and feverishly sought but which cannot be clearly seen or grasped. This association implies a relationship among words, images, and death, all of which Spinell should transcend, according to the speaker. The impossibility of this transcendence also appears in this stanza in the reference to "el yeso colorado de los culos / de los ángeles": the word "culos" used in conjunction with the "ángeles" implies that even the seemingly unambiguous, pure images are inextricably tied to the human realm and may have something to hide. The overall effect of the stanza is thus the communication of the frustration of the search with words and images, for a meaning beyond words and beyond images.

This impossibility appears as the negation of sound in the following stanza:

1 / Framing the Self in *Dibujo de la muerte*

>Mira: no es el pájaro
>debatiendo su herida en el teclado
>ni es la cuerda que gime ni el antiguo
>sonido de su nombre ni los tilos
>ni el sol sobre la nieve.

>[Look: it is not the bird
>debating its wound on the keyboard
>nor is it the chord that moans nor the ancient
>sound of his name nor the linden-trees
>nor the sun on the snow.]

The music here brings us back to a possible explanation of the first line's "son aquí," and the "pájaro" (the hand playing the piano) relates back to night, water, blood, death, wind, etc., because of the previous mention of "las palomas" flying through the night (wind, hair . . .). The human element, present earlier in the eyes and hair that formed part of the night and the water, is represented here by the "teclado," human art. The reappearance of "su nombre" in this stanza evokes its earlier images and elaborates upon them: the "antiguo / sonido de su nombre" is associated here with music and with the "son" of the first stanza, a sound that was beneath death and beneath "su nombre" in the third stanza. Here, that sound is denied, along with the history ("el antiguo / sonido de su nombre") and images, suggesting again that we cannot represent what is beyond human experience. Finally, the "sol sobre la nieve" complicates the process of association even more, since it alludes neither to *Death in Venice* nor to *Tristan*, but, rather, to the chapter entitled "Snow" from Mann's *Magic Mountain* and thereby brings the imagery of that novel into play as well.

The following stanzas continue the process of metonymic association and negation that will become progressively more important. The confusion caused by the metonymic association of images and the multiple allusions is heightened by the lack of punctuation in these lines: the words are not even separated grammatically; hence, the reader's sense of their interconnectedness is heightened. The confluence of images and words reaches its climax at the end of the first section of the poem, the moment that parallels Aschenbach's return to Venice in Mann's novella:

>El afilado
>grito desde la nieve, desde el hueco
>bramido de la noche los zapatos

de viaje deprisa aquel sonido como el largo
vuelo de las gaviotas, allí tienes
Detlev Spinell deprisa la capa
de viaje tu muerte pronto, tienes
que llegar
        el sombrero de los músicos
la pasarela, el Lido, las palomas,
und bon jour Euer, Exzellenz!
                la ola
ya está muy lejos, Venecia, tu muerte
Detlev Spinell has sentido el largo
sonido anticipado, ve, tu muerte,
rescata la belleza de su inútil
adolescencia.

(87–88)

[The sharp
scream from the snow, from the hollow
bellow of the night the shoes
for traveling quickly there death
the sand that sound like the long
flight of the gulls, there you have
Detlev Spinell quickly the cape
for traveling your death soon, you have
to arrive
        the hat of the musicians
the boardwalk, el Lido, the pigeons,
und bon jour Euer, Exzellenz!
                the wave
is already far away, Venice, your death
Detlev Spinell you have felt the long,
anticipated sound, go, your death,
recover the beauty of his useless
adolescence.]

The urgency of the journey is suggested by the sparse punctuation, which encourages the reader to hurry along with the speaker. The frequent use of enjambment serves the same purpose, as well as encouraging the further metonymic association of images. For example, in the first stanza quoted above, "la nieve," "el hueco," "el . . . bramido de la noche," "la muerte," "el sonido," and "el vuelo de las gaviotas" are seen as equivalent, interchangeable, inextricably related. These stanzas at the end of the first part of the poem represent the technical climax of that section, in which all images lose their individual, metaphoric identity and become a conjunction of suggestive possibilities that hint at an unknowable meaning under the surface of things. The climax does not, however, yield a revelation—the journey does not end "debajo de la muerte"—but instead produces continued obscurity and confusion.

As in "Ávila," the second part of "Muerte en Venecia" presents a speaker's reflections on the limitations of the artistic creation of the first part. Significantly, the speaker of this poem contemplates the limitations of language, the principal tool of a literary artist like Thomas Mann. We see here repeated negations of transcendence, the inability to reach "el mismo fondo de los derrumbaderos de la noche" [the very depths of the precipices of the night] or to "rozar la mano ligeramente sobre las aguas / para tocar con los dedos la punta de otros dedos" [brush my hand lightly over the waters / to touch with my fingers the tips of other fingers]. This limitation is linked explicitly to language, as the speaker repeats, "casi podría decirte" [I could almost tell you]. The speaker is left on the "brocal de los pozos" [border of the wells], where he can only contemplate the reflection of his face on the surface of the water (the night, the blood, the wind, the keyboard, the word).

The inextricable meaning of the world and the limitations of (self-)representation are further suggested by the intertextuality of the poem. I have already mentioned the three works by Thomas Mann to which this poem alludes: the title and many images are taken from *Death in Venice*; the character Detlev Spinell and references to music are from *Tristan;* and the snow is from *The Magic Mountain*. The images in the poem are not, however, derived exclusively from Thomas Mann. The second part of the poem is also reminiscent of mystical writings, and particularly of San Juan de la Cruz: for example, the speaker says, "quiero descender blandamente hacia la más alta noche" (89) [I want to descend softly toward the highest night]. The mirror image (the surface of the water) is also typical of mystical writings, but in this poem that transcendent experience is denied. Other images—"muerte," "noche," "pájaros," "ojos," and images of the water's depths—are repeated and developed throughout Carnero's work. This combination of direct and indirect allusions hints at the limited originality of any text by highlighting the inexhaustible intertextuality of literary discourse.

These multiple allusions also expose the effects of intertextuality on personal identity. An initial problem in the poem is the identification of the speaker of the first part, who seeks to lure the reader and Detlev Spinell to the edge of the abyss that he is contemplating. Is he Aschenbach (the protagonist of *Death in Venice*), Hans Castorp (the protagonist of *The Magic Mountain*), a voice within Detlev Spinell himself, Thomas Mann, or the implied author of this poem, a reader of Mann's works and the speaker of the second part of the poem? All of these possibilities could be justified. The imagery suggests that it is Aschenbach, but both Spinell and Aschenbach are personae of Mann. Spinell is a culturalist artist, used satirically in *Tristan*, according to the author, to represent "that lifeless preciosity of the aesthete which I consider supremely dangerous."[13] Aschenbach, a writer and the protagonist of *Death in Venice*, represents a different aspect of Mann's character, dominated by "a 'neoclassical' principle, with a strongly ethical, educative, and humanistic coloring."[14] In the second part of the poem, the speaker is also related to Hans Castorp, the protagonist of *The Magic Mountain*, who, in the chapter "Snow," ventures into the void and finds horror, sacrifice, blood, and death beneath the image of the sublime. Like Castorp, the speaker of "Muerte en Venecia" does not find the ultimate beauty but the ultimate horror "debajo de la muerte": this horror is the intranscendence of human existence and art.

Carnero evokes all of these characters in "Muerte en Venecia": the culturalist aesthete, his more humanistic successor, and the horrified Castorp.[15] However, he is also evoked by them, as was Mann, since "Guillermo Carnero" is a culturalist artist like Spinell; the critic "Guillermo Carnero" studies both the neoclassical and high-modernist periods and thus recalls Aschenbach and Mann; and "Guillermo Carnero," the author of *Dibujo de la muerte*, represents only horror behind the mask of the sublime. My use of quotation marks in this paragraph highlights one of the effects of the relationship between the speaker, the Mann characters, and the creator of this text: a "real" person comes to be considered on the same plane as "fictional characters." Like them, he is constituted of chance intertextual and linguistic connections that do not form a coherent, unified self.

This complexity is also apparent in the relationships among the speakers and the readers in and of this poem. Whatever his identity, the speaker controls, or seeks to control, another figure in the poem, to lure him to his glory or his death. It seems in the first part of the poem that he is beckoning Spinell and the reader, whom he invites to join him in the realm beyond death, beyond words, beyond the world. At the same time, however, the speaker is also a reader, as evidenced by his profound knowledge of the works of Thomas Mann, and the reader who hopes to glimpse some of this metonymic web had best be a reader of Mann as well. This connection between the reader and the fragmented speaker suggests that both are constructed by often random intertextualities.

The concerns and techniques of this poem are explicitly postmodernist. For example, the speaker's failure to reach beyond the world is explicitly linked to the limitations of language: the speaker repeats "casi podría decirte" [I could almost tell you], and silence is the dominant motif of these lines.[16] And, as we saw in the first part, the form of "Muerte en Venecia" is based on contiguity, the chance encounter between words and images. Again, Conte explains that in the postmodern serial, "the poem is a network, a construct in which signs . . . exist in a contiguous relationship with other signs . . . and a paradigmatic relationship with dissimilar but related signs elsewhere in the text", and, in this case, outside the text as well.[17] In sum, "Muerte en Venecia" undermines the concepts of a transcendent meaning, a unified self, and an authoritative text by highlighting the random construction of those multiple frames that create the illusion of essence but that, like the layers of an onion, conceal no core. And, as in "Avila," the unmasking extends beyond the text to authoritative figures, to the poet, to the reader.

"Les charmes de la vie" also demonstrates the limits of interpretation and representation, their imperfect correspondence to an infinitely complex universe, through the metonymic confluence of imagery, allusion, and the perspective of an artist/speaker. This poem, however, focuses more explicitly on the ambiguous position of the artist in relation to the society he represents (both artistically and personally). The allusion in the first part of the poem to the paintings of Watteau (which in turn refer to the Italian and French comedies of the late seventeenth and early eighteenth centuries) suggests immediately the overlapping of "art" and "reality," since Watteau's work so often presents a confusion between dramatic representation and social interaction. This confusion also appears in images that seem to point simultaneously to the surface of reality—the various representations—and the unsoundable depths. Finally, the ambiguous position of the speaker underscores the interrelationship of opposing elements: as director of the drama described in this poem, he controls the representation of society there; however, he is also controlled by it because he forms part of the drama of his day and depends on the very society he criticizes for his success. What is more, he and his work will die with that society; as "Avila" suggested, the interpreted meaning of artistic works is not eternal.

The imagery of "Les charmes de la vie" serves largely to blur the distinctions between art and reality, between light and darkness, between the surface of the world and the unreachable or nonexistent depths below. The first part of the poem sets the stage for the enactment of a comedy, but it soon seems that this performance will take place in society itself. The stage is to be set in such a way as to eliminate all traces of "real life," in the form of birds, in favor of the traditional symbols of artifice. The references to such rich materials as silk and velvet suggest that the stage will be thus set in an opulent upper-class theater. However, the presence of music and the reference to the twirling bodies in a waltz suggest that this comedy will not take place in a theater at all but at the aristocrats' ball. By describing the dance as a drama on the stage, these lines suggest that the dancers will be performing, that the ritual of the waltz is in itself a kind of comedy, and that the interaction among the participants is equally staged. This confusion suggests that "real people" are actors as well who represent different roles in society.[18]

The use of enjambment underscores the implied connection between reality and representation; however, it suggests that there is an underlying meaning that is linked to the surface but hidden by its forms, by the very act of interpretation.

> Que no turben las aves el crepúsculo.
> Va a comenzar el vals. Que todo quede
> en tinieblas. Que las sedas oculten
> las abiertas ventanas, y que alguien desenlace
> los gruesos terciopelos. Nada debe
> amenazar el flujo de la música:
> ningún arista o mármol o pájaro dormido.
> Que nada permanezca.
>
> (95)

> [Do not allow the birds to disturb the sunset.
> The waltz is going to begin. Keep everything
> in darkness. Have the silks conceal
> the open windows, and have someone untie
> the heavy velvets. Nothing should
> threaten the flow of music:
> no arris or marble or sleeping bird.
> Let nothing remain.]

When we reach the end of a verse, we see a transcendent meaning lurking behind the description of the play, but the beginning of the following verse

1 / Framing the Self in *Dibujo de la muerte*

returns us to the surface of things, to the comedy. For example, when we read "Que todo quede," we think about the possibility of immortality, but when we finish the sentence "Que todo quede / en tinieblas," we are transported back to the performance at hand and to the limitations of human life. Similarly, "que las sedas oculten" suggests a social criticism by implying that the show of wealth is hiding something, whereas "que las sedas oculten / las abiertas ventanas" seems to be a simple stage direction. By the time we reach "Que nada permanezca," we automatically read on two levels: let nothing remain on the stage or in life. This technique suggests that the two levels coexist: what appears in the frivolous comedy may contain some deeper meaning, but what appears to be profound may be nothing but a meaningless show. The act of representation simultaneously reveals and blurs meaning.

The unresolved contradiction also appears in the metonymic associations among apparently conflicting images. The images associated with the surface and with art are inextricably linked but not equated to those representing hidden or transcendent meaning. This relationship becomes especially evident in the following lines:

> Sólo el aire
> ilumine las fuentes ocultas de la noche,
> difunda en las estancias un resbalar de remos
> en los estanques, prenda el roce de las hojas
> que desordena el viento entre las alamedas,
> apague los destellos sobre los ventanales,
> que las cortinas pongan su caliente aleteo
> sobre cada cristal, para que los espejos
> no descubran de dónde brotan los surtidores,
> para que no resbalen hacia las balaustradas
> las serpientes del agua, para que en la penumbra
> los colores del mármol y de los terciopelos
> desprendan un ingrávido gorgotear de luces. . . .

(95)

> [Only the air
> should illuminate the hidden fountains of the night,
> diffuse in the rooms a slipping of oars
> in the ponds, capture the rustling of the leaves
> that the wind disorders among the poplar groves,
> turn off the flashes over the large windows,

> have the curtains put their warm fluttering
> over every crystal, so that the mirrors
> may not discover from where the fountain springs,
> so that the serpents of water do not slide
> toward the balustrades, so that in the semidarkness
> the colors of the marble and of the velvets
> give off a delicate gurgling of lights. . . .]

At first glance it appears that the air represents the power that will reveal the hidden meaning when, as ordered, it shines forth to erase the shadows of ignorance and to reveal the "fuentes ocultas." At the same time that the air illuminates, however, it will darken the room, "apague los destellos," and the light is also associated with the surface glitter. The curtains cover the windows to impede reflection, "para que los espejos / no descubran de dónde brotan los surtidores." Furthermore, we see that the image of water as the source of meaning is undermined by its association with the light of the theater: "los colores del mármol y de los terciopelos / desprendan un ingrávido *gorgotear* de luces." The water is also related to the mirrors, for both reflect the light on the surface. This association between light, the theater, mirrors, and water, made as it is in the stage directions for the waltz, implies that the surface will always be taken for the essence of life, that there will be no discovery of "las fuentes ocultas." Even if those wells exist within each of the dancers, they will only reflect further the surface glitter.

The allusion to Watteau's work, beginning in the title of the poem and in the epigraph, largely explains the lifelessness of the dancers, who are literally "statuesque" in this poem, and the confusion between "art" and "reality." Like Carnero, Watteau underscores the artificiality of human existence by implicitly equating courtesans and actors, and by occasionally representing a work of art with more vitality than the human figures. For example *Les Charmes de la Vie* portrays courtesans (or are they actors?) on an outdoor stage vaguely listening to a musician's chords, and *The Shepherds* depicts a group of elegantly dressed courtesans pretending to be shepherds. In both of these paintings, people are pretending to be what they are not by imitating superficial characteristics: actors dress up to look like courtesans and imitate the life the wealthy seem to lead, and courtesans dress like shepherds to participate in the imagined joys of that seemingly simpler life. Furthermore, by setting these two paintings out of doors, Watteau converts nature into a stage, thereby implying that the ritual of comedy is not limited to the theater, that people are constantly performing.

When he refers to other works of art, especially theater, Watteau highlights the superficiality of the situations depicted and the lifelessness of the actors, thereby implying that the reflection of a lifeless society must also be stilted and superficial. Art therefore becomes yet another mirror reflecting the sequins, the surface of the water, the brilliant light of the waltz. In Carnero's poem, as in Watteau's paintings, "reality," "artist," and "art" are interpretive creations, constructed and limited by the social and cultural context that forms them, rather than the reflection of an ideal essence.[19]

The reference to Watteau highlights another important characteristic of this poem: the ambiguous position of the artist in regard to both his social context and art. The use of the imperative mode in this poem points inevitably to the presence of a director, someone who is setting the stage for the performance. It seems that the director of this comedy is the artist, who sets the stage in his work with images and controls all the action that takes place there. This role places the artist in the same position as an authoritarian ruler because he seems to absolutely control his subjects' lives with language, restricting their freedom, preventing them from finding a profound meaning for their lives beyond the mirrors in which they are reflected. The people become twirling puppets under authoritarian direction, and the person who controls language holds the strings.

That control is not as absolute as it seems, however; for, despite his apparent aloofness and superiority, the artist must necessarily inhabit the same world as his subjects, and he is equally circumscribed by its rules. He participates in the drama as its director (in the painting as its creator; in the poem as its author), and, ironically, he depends for its success upon the very people he seeks to control and criticize in it. Someone, after all, must be his subject, the censors must allow him to publish or sell his work, and someone must pay him. Furthermore, as part of the society he paints, he must necessarily reflect some of its values and beliefs in his work. He therefore cannot completely control the world he depicts, nor can he transcend it, because he relies upon it for his subject matter, for his vision, and for his livelihood.

In the second part of the poem, the artist's integral ties to his society become apparent through the speaker's ruminations about Anacreon's work while he continues to observe the waltz. Here the speaker seems to accept his subjects' superficiality and his own as a gesture of despair. He asks, why bother looking for transcendence, why protest injustice, if all is lost? One might as well enjoy oneself, join the waltz, and not worry about meaning:

> Anacreonte supo renunciar a casi todos los mitos de su tiempo:
> patria, fama, triunfo, dignidad de soldado,
> respeto hacia los muertos y amistad con los dioses.
> ¿Cómo no serenarse, si todo está perdido?
>
> (96)

> [Anacreon knew to renounce almost all the myths of his time:
> nation, fame, triumph, soldier's dignity,
> respect for the dead, and friendship with the gods.
> Why not be calm, if all is lost?]

These lines suggest that one can only detach oneself from society's values if that society has already perished, if its vision has become fragmented and the values meaningless. This lack of integrity appears in the final lines of the poem, in which the speaker seems to accept that the superficiality of the social waltz is unavoidable and that he might as well join in willingly:

> Ahora resbala por las escalinatas
> la múltiple aureola de las luces
> (¿Y por qué no subir, si todo está perdido?)
> y se desgrana el vals entre las risas
> mientras las lentejuelas de las máscaras
> reflejan un brillante remolino de sedas,
> como un enorme espejo alucinado.
>
> (97)

> [Now slipping around the grand staircases is
> the multiple aureole of the lights
> (And why not rise, if all is lost?)
> and the waltz becomes unstrung amidst the laughter
> while the sequins of the masks
> reflect a brilliant whirling of silks,
> like an enormous hallucinatory mirror.]

On the surface we see only a reflection of a reflection, myriad reflections of meaningless glitter. We cannot know what, if anything, is behind the sequined mask, because our only tools for discovering that hidden meaning are art and language, which reflect the human world, and that world is necessarily superficial. In other words, because he is part of the society he depicts, the artist sees his own face reflected in the fragmented, glittering surface.

1 / Framing the Self in *Dibujo de la muerte* 49

Like "Avila" and "Muerte en Venecia," "Les charmes de la vie" demonstrates the contextual nature of art, identity, and knowledge, their inextricable ties to the society that produces them. Here, the speaker, identified with Watteau, represents and criticizes his society through a series of images that confound the artificial and the real. His use of the imperative, however, combined with his introspective musings concerning the superficiality of society and art, reveals that he, like his subjects, is trapped on the surface, with no passage to a deeper meaning free of the context in which he lives and creates. He is simultaneously in control of and controlled by the society he commands.

The techniques of metonymy, allusion, and the use of a speaker who is an artist or artistic creation, an "analogous historical personage," as well as the motifs of silence, of submerged, lost meaning, and of masks covering a void, are repeated throughout *Dibujo de la muerte*, providing the book with a coherence that the various titles—"Castilla," "Primer día de verano en Wragby Hall" [First day of summer in Wragby Hall"], "Bacanales en Rimini para olvidar a Isotta" [Bacchanalia in Rimini to forget Isotta]—seem to belie. The connections to "Avila," "Muerte en Venecia" and "Les charmes de la vie" are sometimes apparent. The allusions may be the same—"Watteau en Nogent-Sur-Marne" refers to the same artist as "Les charmes de la vie" and also describes a waltz; the statues in "Avila" are reminiscent of those in "Les charmes de la vie" and Mann's *Magic Mountain*—or the images may recur: the twirling bodies and mirrors reappear in "El movimiento continuo" [Continuous motion], the fountains and the night in "Galería de retratos" [Portrait gallery], the dizzying artistic reflections of reflections framing the speaker and mirroring emptiness and death in "El altísimo Juan Sforza compone unos loores a su dama mientras César Borgia marcha sobre Pésaro" [The Most Exalted Juan Sforza composes eulogies to his lady while Caesar Borgia marches upon Pesaro].[20] Everywhere we see beauty, art, masks, silence and death. Most often, however, it is the technique that links these works. The metonymic association among images and works weaves a net, weaves a spell, casts a spell and a net, around and over the reader, who is drawn into the search like Detlev Spinell, like Aschenbach, like Castorp, and cast off like Watteau, like Anacreon, like all of Mann's characters, like all of Carnero's speakers. The search for submerged meaning is fruitless, frustrated by the stubborn resistance of the surface, which inevitably reflects only our own faces, the identities and the meanings constructed by our contexts. The speakers and the readers share this struggle, which leads them to give in and join the waltz glittering in the mirrors—

"¿Cómo no serenarse si todo está perdido?"—and to resist, like Spinell and Aschenbach, like the speaker in "Watteau en Nogent-Sur-Marne," who asks, "Pero los aprendidos pasos de baile, ¿son acaso / razón para una vida?" (99) [But the learned dance steps, can they be / the reason for a life?]. These seemingly opposing choices are really very similar, for those who give in and, like Watteau, serve as a mirror to a superficial society still reflect its defects, and those, like Aschenbach and Detlev Spinell, who seek the submerged meaning (sound or eyes) see only a reflection of the surface and of themselves on the surface—"he visto despacio el opaco vacío de mis ojos" (88) [I have seen slowly the opaque vacuum of my eyes]. *Dibujo de la muerte* is a sketch of the artist's relationship to his surroundings and his readers. It shows that the creator is also a creation, a product of a "created reality," his social, historical, and artistic context. It is a rendering of the death that is human life, lived on the surface only, tied to a context and thus condemned to oblivion. It is a mirror reflecting a mirror reflecting only sequins and frames, a reflection of the reflection of a void.

2
A Question of Authority:
El sueño de Escipión

AFTER the rich, elusive images and the elaborate, allusive references of *Dibujo de la muerte*, the directness and brevity (fifteen poems rather than twenty-six) of Carnero's second book, *El sueño de Escipión* (1971) [Scipio's dream], may come as a surprise to the reader. The speaker tells us outright that the subject matter of these poems is the act of discourse itself, the methodology of poetry and the role of the poet, as in the poem "El sueño de Escipión":

> El poema procede de la realidad
> por vía de violencia; realidad viene a ser
> visualizar un caos desde una perspectiva
> que el poeta preside desde el punto de fuga.
>
> (152)[1]

> [The poem proceeds from reality
> by means of violence; reality comes to mean
> visualizing a chaos from a perspective
> over which the poet presides from the vanishing point.]

Despite this seeming transparency, however, *El sueño de Escipión* is a complex elaboration of the ideas, images, and techniques presented in *Dibujo de la muerte*. The poems in this book continue to explore the problematic relationship between the world, the poet, the text, and the reader through the use of metonymy and allusion, and through the focus on the speaker; and they continue to tie artistic issues to broad philosophical questions beyond the text. The differences lie in the choice of images—with the exception of those previously elaborated in *Dibujo*, they are mostly related to literary creation—and in the more ironic representation of literary history and of the author as power figure.

This poetry indeed invites us to question authority by revealing the profound vulnerability of language and of those who employ language to sustain authorial power. It raises this issue first by discussing and demonstrating the illimitable referentiality of language: if no word is the original (or the final) word, then the authority the word represents must also be only partial and provisional. This concept was represented primarily through the predominance of metonymy in *Dibujo de la muerte*; in *El sueño de Escipión* it is suggested in part through the allusion to those metonymies in the "miradas sin pupila" [looks without pupils], "decorados de teatro" [theater settings], and "un mar escondido" [a secret sea] of "Jardín inglés" (129–33) [English garden], in the birds of "Elogio de Linneo" (135) [Eulogy for Linneus], "Erótica del marabú" (136) [Erotics of the marabou] and "Oda a Algernon Charles Swinburne" (150) [Ode to Algernon Charles Swinburne] and in the images of death. And we recall the entire earlier book when we encounter three allusions to its title: a painting is a "dibujo de la muerte" [sketch of death] in "Jardín inglés"; Orpheus's song is a "dibujo de la muerta" [sketch of the dead woman] in "Ineptitud de Orfeo y alabanza de Alceste" (137) [Orpheus's ineptitude and Alcestis's praise]; and the inadequacy of art is described in "Rodéanos de rápidos desnudos" (145) [Surround us with rapid nudes] in the following manner:

> Y así el retorno del dibujo
> es fuga del color, su recurrir
> para ausencia y ficción, como su eco.

> [And thus the return of the sketch
> is the flight of color, its recurrence
> for absence and fiction, like its echo.]

Upon reading these words, readers familiar with Carnero's work may recall the indeterminacy and interconnectedness of the images in *Dibujo de la muerte*, and the frustration of the poet who sought to snare meaning in his metonymic webs and was left with only those webs and the reflection of his own face on the surface of the void. This intertextuality with Carnero's prior book allows us to delve more deeply into the problems delineated there without having to retrace our steps: *El sueño de Escipión* is, in relation to *Dibujo de la muerte*, "fuga del color, su recurrir / para ausencia y ficción, como su eco." We may now consider the problems of interpretation, representation, identity, and control without the color of the first book, not in the metonymic webs of images, texts, and speakers but in the individual word, poem, and speaker, which are plurivalent in themselves, constituted of innumerable intertextual connections.

El sueño de Escipión demonstrates the ramifications of this plurality on the authority of the poet, who seeks to control his poetic and personal worlds but who finds himself circumscribed by the limitations imposed by readers, language, poetic structure, literary history, and the referents of his discourse.[2] All of the poems of this book explore some aspect of literary representation and reception, through the relationships between texts ("Chagrin d'amour principe d'oeuvre d'art," "El sueño de Escipión,"), between writers and reality ("Chagrin d'amour," "Ineptitud"), between writers and their texts ("Ineptitud," "Rodéanos"), between texts and reality ("Jardín inglés," "Chagrin d'amour"), between texts and readers ("El sueño de Escipión," "Ineptitud"), between readers and writers ("Erótica del marabú"), and between writers, readers, texts, and reality ("Investigación de una doble metonimia" (144) [Investigation of a double metonymy]). This exploration draws attention to the boundaries between authors, texts, and readers, and it destabilizes textual and authorial power by revealing their mechanisms and by encouraging multiplicity and free play—that is, the transgression of those boundaries.

The slippery play of textual power is suggested by the allusions in these poems, which create and undermine authorial power. In *Sueño*, for example, other authors are often cited in scholarly footnotes in order to legitimize the speaker's own authority. However, the contradictions between these equally authoritative Western sources foregrounds the uncertainty of proof itself and the instability of the seemingly monolithic history of Western philosophy.[3] The speaker's procedure here reveals that knowledge is constituted in the Western critical tradition through the defense of partial theories by interested individuals with the use of unreliable proof. Lyotard explains the traditional establishment of scientific claims in a similar manner: "[A]s long as I can produce proof, it is permissible to think that reality is the way I say it is."[4] It is permissible but not necessary, and the counterproofs cited in these poems reveal that the claims of all authors are falsifiable; that is, they are not essentially but only provisionally true.[5] This instability reveals the contingency of authorial power, which depends on unverifiable prior arguments (the history of aesthetic theory and practice, the bibliography).

The author's power is also contingent upon the cooperation and skill of readers. First of all, the author must rely upon readers' approval for his reputation and livelihood. What is more, he cannot control their use or interpretations of his poems. The author of these texts (often identified with the speaker) must take for granted that his readers will recognize his many references to artistic figures of the Western world (or, at least, that they will be able and inclined to research), and that they will agree with his interpretations of those figures. As I said above, however, he shows in the poems that learned readers often disagree and that interpretation often depends on the cultural and temporal contexts of the reader. This sort of interpretive freedom must extend to the poems of *El sueño de Escipión*, as well as to the texts cited in them. The speaker also recognizes that the instability of the sign gives the reader some interpretive power over the text. Thus, the allusions, in conjunction with the metapoetical musings of the speaker, reveal that, although the poet does exercise some control over readers, that control is contingent upon a historical tradition, a narrow definition of the linguistic sign, and the readers' cooperation.[6]

In these ways, this book places into question the very concept of the author.[7] The reflections of the poet in and on the text mark a differentiation between the author as person and the author as constituted by his texts. According to Michel Foucault, the "author" is not simply a person who writes; rather, "author" denotes a certain intellectual status, endowed upon the implied writer of a unified, high-quality corpus of texts. In other words, the author is not the "real writer," who may or may not maintain such a level of personal and creative consistency, but an "author-function," constituted by discourse. The effect of this author-function is to limit the plurality of signification by reducing the interpretive possibilities of a text to the definitions afforded by the unified work of an individual author. The poems in *El sueño de Escipión* gradually "kill" that kind of author, a process that culminates in the poem "El sueño de Escipión," in which the speaker participates as both reader and poet in the unending process of textual signification.

The ambiguous nature of poetic power is the explicit focus of "Erótica del marabú," a poem in which the poet is portrayed as a powerful sacred bird, a cruel and repulsive creature, a victim of its portrayal, and ultimately an object of consumption.

> Mirad el marabú, el pájaro sagrado.
> Escruta el devenir, busca marsupio
> en la tragedia,
> degusta la carroña, picotea cucuyos,
> cuando regresa al nido con el buche bien lleno
> pliega las alas VED el valioso plumón,

2 / A Question of Authority: *El sueño de Escipión*

    escruta el devenir es el sagrado
    avizora los ojos de los muertos
    los deglute, no es un animal tierno
    y sin embargo véla a la luz de su buche
    zancas de marabú, pico amarillo,
    torpes inclinaciones olfatorias,
    su digerir es una ontología,
    plumas negruzcas, en plumonpoemas,
    el valioso plumón para el aposteriori
    y exhibiciones-de-las-damas.
                                                   (136)

    [Look at the marabou, the sacred bird.
    He scrutinizes the past, he looks for a marsupial
    in the tragedy,
    he samples carrion, he nibbles beetles,
    when he returns to the nest with his belly full
    he folds its wings SEE his valuable plumule
    he scrutinizes the future he is the sacred one
    he observes the eyes of the dead
    he eats them, he is not a tender animal
    and yet look at him in the light of his belly
    long stork legs, yellow bill,
    clumsy olfactory inclinations,
    his digestion is an ontology,
    blackish plumes, in plumepoems,
    the valuable plumule for the a posteriori
    and exhibitions-of-the-ladies.]

The metapoetic focus of this poem, suggested especially by the conversion of plumes into poems in the antepenultimate verse, invites us to analyze the nature of the poet, the readers, and the referent. The poem presents the poet as both a sacred bird and a revolting one, revealing society's ambivalent feelings toward him: it both reveres and despises him because he does not respect its traditions. This ambivalence derives from the double positioning of members of society, who are both the referents of the poem, "la carroña," and its readers. This duality is even represented linguistically: the readers are addressed in both the plural ("Mirad," "VED") and singular ("véla") forms.

    The poet's position relative to society is also ambivalent, since he sets himself apart from his context in order to scrutinize it but relies upon it for his sustenance and raw material. It seems that the poet, isolated by his nature from the mainstream of society, is free to pick it apart, for he is not limited by his fear of public opinion. This freedom and this criticism give him a form of power over society; thus, he feels superior to those he devours. At the same time, however, he is dependent upon literary critics and literate readers for his exalted position and, indeed, for his survival. Furthermore, once he has sold his poems, they are appropriated by the very society they criticized, becoming "el valioso plumón para el aposteriori / y exhibiciones-de-las-damas." Still, despite the apparent conversion of his poems into objects for social consumption, the poet does not completely lose his power, for this rare bird remains the focus of the readers' attention, even in this poem, where the commands to the readers—"Mirad," "VED," "véla"—keep the poet's control at the center of our attention.

The double position of the poet, simultaneously inside and outside of his social context, and at the center and at the margin of our attention, is also represented in the framing mechanism of this poem. The "poet" is both the object of this poem and its subject—he is the referent and the speaker—apparently within the text and outside of it. If we extend the implications of this duality, along with the considerations of the author's limitations in this poem, we may conclude that "Guillermo Carnero" occupies a similar role; that is, he is both within and without this text. The metapoetic focus of this poem, then, along with its framing device, allows us to consider the artificiality of the concept of "author," in the Foucauldian sense of a unified self wholly identified with a unified literary corpus. Even further, we may consider that "authority" is imbued with power by those doubly positioned as readers and referents. It is finally impossible to discern which party is more powerful—the merciless marabou that digests society to produce the poem or that society which determines his economic and artistic future and appropriates his poems for decorative use.

"Investigación de una doble metonimia" also explores the complex play of power between writers and readers, as well as the limitations of representation; again, the explicit focus on the poetic act reveals the power of the authorial figure. Here, readers complicate the problematic relationship between text and referent, since their multiple interpretations may open seemingly closed texts, thereby unraveling the structured order imposed by the poet.

> Quien concibió la gloria de estos muros
> amaba más la vida.

2 / A Question of Authority: *El sueño de Escipión*

      La elevación del cerro
revela y rige la función del lago:
invertir las imágenes y su apariencia plácida.
El negro nigromante al umbral de la gruta,
el eremita, la sombra de Quirón
acordando su andar como se ignoran.
Del otro lado la concreta estampa
sin la indulgencia de la alegoría
pero más esplendor; los encajes del hierro,
el jardincillo de los Conciertos Sacros,
la tenue batahola de la máquina hidráulica
que suenan para ti.
      La música distante
las risas y el sudor y la reyerta
nunca serán tu historia
y suenan para ti.
      Tu sangre crece
no en la persecución, por su relato,
y así desdices sombras que sin tú conocerlas
habitan ante ti, no su despojo
que despierta su carne.
      Y hasta inventas
para asirlas extremos
de precisa dicción, es tu literatura
no menos conocida, perseguidor de sombras,
retórico brillante
en tu recinto oscuro.
      Y tuvo libertad.

(144)

[Whoever conceived the glory of these walls
loved life more.
      The elevation of the ridge
reveals and rules the function of the lake:
to invert the images and their placid appearance.
The black black-magician at the threshold of the grotto
the hermit, the shadow of Chiron,
remembering his movement as they ignore it.
On the other side the concrete stamp
without the indulgence of allegory
but more splendor; the iron grooves,
the little garden of the Sacred Concerts,

>   the tenuous clatter of the hydraulic machine
>   that sounds for you.
> 					The distant music
>   the laughter and the sweat and the brawl
>   will never be your (hi)story
>   and sound for you.
> 					Your blood surges
>   not in the pursuit, in the relating of it,
>   and thus you unsay shadows that without your knowing them
>   live before you, not their spoils
>   which awaken your flesh.
> 					And you even invent
>   in order to grasp them extremes
>   of precise diction, your literature is
>   no less known, pursuer of shadows,
>   brilliant rhetorician
>   in your dark enclosure.
> 					And he was free.]

The title of the poem and its form exercise a kind of control over readers, who must try to find the double metonymy and make sense of the structure in their interpretive efforts. These two techniques invite closure. It is apparent that the first two lines and the last line of the poem, which describe a third person, create a frame around the intervening verses, which describe a "tú," who is thereby structurally delimited or encircled. The search for the double metonymy also implies the possibility of closing the hermeneutic circle: we could say, for example, that the chain of images referring to the poem forms one metonymy, and the images describing the referent form the other. We could even say that the structure reflects the metonymic relationship between the poem and its referent: the frame would be like the "cerro," dividing the poem ("el lago") from "reality," and the middle section the inverted mirror image that is art.

It seems, however, that this closure is illusory, because it does not take into account other metonymic constructions and connections implicit in the text and in language itself. For example, within the middle section, which, according to the interpretation above, represents the poetic inversion of reality, we find words—"la concreta estampa," "los encajes del hierro," "el jardincillo de los Conciertos Sacros," "la máquina hidráulica"—that seek to represent the "real," that which is outside the literary. In linguistic terms, this technique suggests that the individual word is only metonymically connected to the referent, and that the referent itself is tied to our interpretation of it: thus "el jardincillo" does not simply represent the object, but also, in part, an interpretation of it. If that is the case, then it is impossible to close an interpretation; each word will reopen it. What is more, the coexistence of these apparently unconnected words denoting "real objects" within a stanza of a poem creates metonymic connections among them, inviting further interpretation.

The structure of the poem and the numerous references to creators in the middle section of the poem may also suggest that the poet, as well as the referent, cannot be fully represented in the text, since poetic form delimits the representation of the innumerable connections that constitute identity. The structure of this poem suggests that the same is true for the reader, because it creates a contiguous relationship not only between the poem and the referent, the frame, and the center but also between the reader and the text, and the poet and the text. As we saw in *Dibujo de la muerte,* the poet and the reader may also be described as fictional, metonymic constructs, and the poem may be the "cerro" that links and divides them; thus both reader and poet are reflected and inverted in the poem. What is more, when readers reflect upon the poem, they bring their own personal and literary experiences to bear upon their interpretations of it, creating yet another metonymic chain that multiplies the double bind implied by the title and the structure, and loosens the boundaries of the text.

The longer poems in *El sueño de Escipión*—"Jardín inglés," "Chagrin d'amour principe d'oeuvre d'art," and "El sueño de Escipión"—expose the problems of authority by tracing the poetic process and apparently allowing us to "observe" the poet as he seeks to use language to transform everyday reality into art. These poems foreground the contradictions of literary creation, of language, and of the author, and these contradictions allow us to question authorial power even as we experience it.

The poet as a human, yet power-wielding, oddity is the focus of "Chagrin d'amour principe d'oeuvre d'art," a poem whose ostensible theme is the insufficiency of pure poetry. This poem describes the process of the poetic recreation of "reality" and, in so doing, highlights the insecurity and self-interest of the poet and the provisionality of his and his text's authority. The speaker of the poem is a poet who discusses his own aesthetic development—the change from a kind of realism to Neoplatonism to metapoetry, which represents some mixture of the other two: "el dominio / de la palabra, el alma / de las cosas" [the dominion / of the word, the soul / of things]. He asserts that this final phase is the most authentic. He hopes to prove his point through the straightforward, logical, and scholarly elaboration of its merits, citing authorities where needed to support his case and alluding to other authors as a contrast to his own views. However, the ironic tone of his self-elaboration and the inclusion of key personal details suggest that the elaborate theoretical argument is a cover for and an escape from some of his weaknesses in the area of human relations. This revelation encourages us to question his sincerity, along with the objectivity and the authority of his scholarly interpretation of human experience.

The allusions in the text are apparently used to support the speaker's arguments, but they often have the opposite effect. First, they weaken his argument by exposing the errors and limitations of all others: if everyone else has failed to elaborate transcendent ideals in their texts, how can this writer hope to succeed? Furthermore, the footnotes reveal the provisional nature of scholarly authority, because they refer to authors from different periods with greatly divergent aesthetic ideas, leaving the reader with unanswered questions. Does the speaker support the views of Marsilio Ficino, an Italian Neoplatonist of the Renaissance, or those of Luis Carrillo y Sotomayor, a Spaniard who sought to justify Gongorism? What is the relationship between Ficino, Plato, and Carrillo y Sotomayor? How do we decide? Who determines authority? The speaker clearly points us to the Western literary and philosophical tradition, but he shows us that it is far from hegemonic or even authoritative, and he thereby undermines his own authorial power, which is derived from that tradition.

"Chagrin d'amour" apparently begins on a note of reality, as the speaker discusses the situation that gave rise to his poetic creation; I say "apparently" because all we have here is a linguistic (re)creation of that referent— "Así tu cuerpo fue." He moves almost immediately to a discussion of the transcendent power of artistic creation:

> Así tu cuerpo fue como resume
> nuestra pupila el mundo: la imagen delicada
> de la belleza basta
> para hacernos sentir, y la pintura
> de la propia desdicha.
> Y la felicidad no tiene historia.
> Pero en la ciudad vive: cada calle
> es un recuerdo que salvar,
> la acuarela del cielo en los días de lluvia

> y otras banalidades de filiación diversa
> que son felicidad.
>
> (140)
>
> [Thus was your body as condenses
> our pupil the world: the delicate image
> of beauty is enough
> to make us feel, and the picture
> of misfortune itself.
> And happiness has no history.
> But in the city it lives: every street
> is a memory to be saved,
> the watercolor of the sky on rainy days
> and other banalities of diverse filiation
> that are happiness.]

The speaker asserts his authorial control by telling his beloved, the referent of his poem, that she is as he interprets her to be, a delicate image of beauty, and that the image, more than the reality, moves us. And, of course, he is right, for we never see the referent, only the poet's re-creation. The poet is, therefore, quite powerful: he preserves her (the beloved, the world, the feeling: the referent) in his art, and he converts life's banalities into meaning; only in art do they become "felicidad." It is apparent that he is confident of his power over reality: the woman has now become a symbol of the referent in general, and she is "dispuesta a despertar a una palabra" [ready to awaken with a word]. The poet will have the last word in this affair, and with that word he will finally be able to control his context.

He soon questions the authenticity of this power, however, for in order to dominate his surroundings, he has had to distance himself emotionally from them. How can he be sure of his authority over reality if he does not fully participate in it? Again, his double positioning undermines his authority.

> Estéril todavía más que la dicha misma acaso
> este poema. Imaginarla
> con la mirada lúcida del constructor de frases,
> perseguir la anuencia de memoria, dicción
> y pensamiento,
> y tener la impudicia de escribirla: bastardos
> los gozos del poeta, como su diosa misma.
>
> (141)

> [Even more sterile perhaps than happiness itself
> this poem. To imagine her
> with the lucid gaze of the constructor of phrases,
> to pursue the consent of memory, diction
> and thought,
> and to have the indecency to write her: bastards
> are the joys of the poet, like his goddess herself.]

The poet's pleasures are illegitimate, like those of Orpheus, who, "al no mirar atrás, cuanto en arte edifica / goza sólo dibujo de la muerta" [because he did not look back, no matter what he constructs in art, / he will enjoy only a sketch of the dead woman] ("Ineptitud"). The poetic act is an exercise of power over the referent, but it is only partially successful: it does not reproduce the referent when it copies and transforms it. The poet cannot give us the referent, but only a construction of language that represents it and does not replace or change it.

The allusion to and criticism of proponents of pure poetry further underscores the limitations of the poetic enterprise. The epigraph, "Le plus triste des alchimistes," quotes Baudelaire in an apparent reference to the condition of one who seeks to convert life into art but inevitably fails. Later in the poem, we find a direct response to the poetry of Claudio Rodríguez, specifically, to *Don de la ebriedad*, where Rodríguez writes:

> Siempre la claridad viene del cielo;
> es un don: no se halla entre las cosas
> sino muy por encima, y las ocupa
> haciendo de ello vida y labor propias.[8]

> [Always clarity comes from the heavens;
> it is a gift: it is not found among things
> but far above them, and it occupies them
> making of that its own life and labor.]

In Rodríguez's poem, the world, including the poem and the self, exists to give form to pure meaning. Carnero's speaker views the poetic process more ironically. He suggests that the poet looks for meaning in the transcendent sphere because he wants to escape from his personal and social limitations:

> La palabra es un don
> para quien nada siente, le asegura
> la existencia de un orden,

2 / A Question of Authority: *El sueño de Escipión*   63

>   el derecho de asilo. Porque él ni mira el mundo
>   ni lo advierte, y sus ojos
>   no son más que un espejo al que conmueve
>   una corporeidad de formas puras:
>   sus goces son la muerte, la renuncia
>   anticipada asiste a su pupila
>   con un halo de ausencia, y su deseo
>   tiene toda la pompa de las causas perdidas:
>   extremo de elegancia
>   y de temor. *Et solus iste sapit.*
>   Porque el amor nos salva: no haber vivido en vano.
>
>   (141)
>
>   [The word is a gift
>   for one who feels nothing, it assures him
>   of the existence of an order,
>   the right to asylum. Because he neither looks at the world
>   nor notices it, and his eyes
>   are no more than a mirror which is moved by
>   a corporeity of pure forms:
>   his pleasures are death, the renunciation
>   foreseen accompanies his pupil
>   with a halo of absence, and his desire
>   has all the pomp of lost causes:
>   an extremity of elegance
>   and fear. *Et solus iste sapit.*
>   Because love saves us: not to have lived in vain.]

The aims of pure poetry are already a lost cause. *"Et solus iste sapit,"* he tells us, quoting Marsilio Ficino (as he tells us in a scholarly footnote). The citation of this Italian writer, who precipitated the influence of a Christianized Plato during the Italian Renaissance with his *Theologia Platonica*, reminds us that poetry does not eternally represent essences and thus underscores the speaker's questioning of pure poetry, his doubts concerning the nature, source, and value of the poetic enterprise.

The remainder of the poem describes the symbiotic relationship between reality and text: life begets art, and art begets life; together they form meaning. Art recreates the often sordid and monotonous referent:

>   Y gracias al poema
>   te llamamos amor. Si no, qué llamaríamos
>   a tu dudoso hechizo,

siempre el poema definiendo
el monótono encuentro con las sábanas sucias,
propiciando sutiles
especies de flaqueza,
ennobleciendo la común astucia
que nos devuelve el mundo, y hasta nos proporciona
razón para crear.

(142)

[And thanks to the poem
we call you love. If not, what would we call
your dubious spell,
always the poem defining
the monotonous encounter between soiled sheets,
propitiating subtle
species of weakness,
ennobling the common cunning
that returns the world to us, and even provides us with
a reason to create.]

But, the poet needs the referent as a starting point for his creation:

Gracias a un cuerpo
apetecer el mundo, y gracias al dolor
(preferimos nombrarlo con más delicadeza)
recobrar el dominio
de la palabra, el alma
de las cosas.

(142)

[Thanks to a body
to crave the world, and thanks to pain
(we prefer to name it with more delicacy)
to recover the dominion
of the word, the soul
of things.]

Neither element dominates the other: language is inadequate ("preferimos nombrarlo con más delicadeza"), and reality is insufficient unless it gives us a means to create. The last three lines of the stanza syntactically and visually equate meaning and language; the appositional construction "el dominio de la palabra" and "el alma de las cosas" implies that they are synonymous, as does the solitary juxtaposition of "palabra" and "alma" in the penultimate line. In these lines, the poet seems to have attained a union between word and essence.

The irony of the last stanza, however, undermines this triumph. The speaker claims here that he is grateful for the painful experience, for it provided him with the raw material with which to weave his text:

> Mirar
> con gratitud inconfesable
> el desenlace de la historia
> porque su esencia es noble; y más, es decorosa
> esa contemplación entre doliente
> y resignada, de antemano
> prevista, que resume
> tanta sabiduría; y como el arte, santa.
>
> (143)

> [To look
> with inconfessable gratitude
> at the denouement of the story
> because its essence is noble; and, even more, it is decorous,
> that contemplation between sorrowful
> and resigned, beforehand
> foreseen, that summarizes
> such wisdom; and like art, holy.]

The speaker seems to have been successful in his attempt to convert life into poetry. Because we have witnessed the poet's failed attempts to master his circumstances, however, his triumphant conclusion is not entirely convincing. Even though he assumes a disinterested and philosophical pose in the first four lines of the stanza, lines 5 through 8 highlight its artificiality, revealing the poet's self-interested (he seeks to eliminate his pain by calling it his inspiration) re-creation of the past. It seems at first that the speaker is bolstering the image of poet as prophet by claiming that he could foresee the result of the relationship's end, and he further elevates himself by claiming sainthood for his contemplation and his poem. This position is undercut, however, by the ironic tone of the stanza, as when the poet calls attention to the superficial artificiality of the poetic pose, calling it "decorosa," or when he congratulates himself for a foresight that he has only attained in retrospect. Once the poet has revealed his humanity and the imperfection of his work, he cannot reclaim divinity, and words like "santa" become more obviously ironic. The mask is gone, and we see the very human manipulation of reality to suit personal needs.

The concluding lines of the poem continue to both reaffirm and undermine the elevated place of the poet. They allude to and reshape those earlier lines of the poem that asserted the creative power of the word:

> Amor, poema, una ciudad por ti
> es un mundo, una justa
> coloración del alba;
> es familiar el brillo de su asfalto
> y sus calles amigas.
> La palabra es un don, y sus goces bastardos
> me dan razón de ti, son tu mejor herencia.
> Pero no sin ficción.

> [Love, poem, a city because of you
> is a world, an exact
> coloration of the dawn;
> how familiar the shine of its asphalt
> and its friendly streets.
> The word is a gift, and its bastard joys
> give me an explanation for you, they are your greatest inheritance.
> But not without fiction.]

The first line takes us back to the lines, "Y gracias al poema / te llamamos amor," which affirmed the power of the poetic word, a stance that is strengthened by the words "justa," "familiar," "brillo," and "amigas." The concluding verses simultaneously assert the power of the poet and reveal his vulnerability, a contradictory posture that has appeared throughout the poem. They refer explicitly to the critique of Rodríguez, pure poetry, and Neoplatonism, specifically to the lines "La palabra es un don / para quien nada siente" and "bastardos / los gozos del poeta, como su diosa misma." The lines simultaneously support the power of poetry, for we see that "don palabra" is not only fecund but rich: his union with reality produces "goces bastardos" and generates meaning—"me dan razón de ti, son tu mejor herencia." The last line of the poem also serves the dual function of undermining and supporting poetic legitimacy. "Pero no sin ficción." Does it mean that words are only prolific if they are literary? Or does it mean that the power of the poet is fictitious because it relies upon the readers' suspension of disbelief and upon the limitation of linguistic meaning through a literary structure—"el dominio / de la palabra, el alma / de las cosas"—that the plurivalence of the individual word undermines? The text supports both interpretations.

In "Chagrin d'amour principe d'oeuvre d'art," then, the poet appears in all his mythic glory, and then is alternately shrunk in stature as the fragility of his power becomes evident and reinflated as we recognize his continued effect upon our perceptions of reality. We see the supposed omniscience of the poet in his grand pronouncements ("Y gracias al poema / te llamamos amor"), in his references to scholars, and in his prophecies (the conclusion was "de antemano prevista"). And we see his apparent omnipotence in relation to his context and his creation: "saberla / dispuesta a despertar a una palabra." The poet's godlike status is undermined, however, by the revelation of his selfish motive—in this case, the desire to diminish his pain by recreating the past in his poem. Once we have witnessed this struggle to manipulate reality, readers can no longer pretend that this is the work of a disinterested and all-knowing god nor even of God's messenger. We are not even left with the solace of transparent and representative language; the wordplay, the multiple allusions to other texts, the quotations taken out of context, and the repetition of words and phrases draw our attention to the provisional relationship between language and the reality it seeks to represent. The revelation that language cannot embody meaning further subverts the poet's control over his poetic world by inviting the reader to play as well and thus to contribute to the creation of the poetic work. Readers are empowered by our realization that the poet's solitary hold on meaning is temporary and, most important, fictitious. We are, however, still affected by the poetic text; it has changed our perception of reality and of poetic creation. The poem reveals the power struggle between poet, referent, readers, and texts and thereby makes us aware of the dynamic nature of power itself.

The ephemeral and illusory control of meaning is the central issue in "El sueño de Escipión," which presents a plurality of poetic voices from Giovanni Cavalcanti in the thirteenth century through Boris Vian and Carnero (or this incarnation of him) in the twentieth. The poem decenters the notion of "author" and "origin" by not following the chronology of the cited texts and by blurring the distinction between "original" and quoted text. The speaker in this poem presents himself as both the reader and the author of the text, and certainly as the creator of the pastiche of quotations, repetitions, commentaries, free translations, and contradictions. Rather than supporting the authority of any single view, this presentation of authors and works from different times and places (many of them comments upon and/or translations of some or all of the others) suggests that this endless re-elaboration of ideas and forms constitutes meaning. In this way, "El sueño de Escipión" kills "the author," the authoritative origin of meaning, and invites readers to resist closure, to challenge the very notion that one definition or set of definitions could eliminate all others.

From the first lines, it is apparent that "El sueño de Escipión" is as much about poetic commentary as about poetry. The first two stanzas refer to Laforgue's theory of poetics and the effect of that theory (and its practice) on our reading of the work of William Shakespeare; they also refer to Polonius's comment on Hamlet's playacting:

> Preguntado Laforgue por el ser del poema:
> *"Ni mon ni mon art, Monsieur"*.
> Lo que supone,
> igual que sus sarcasmos sobre el claro de luna
> hace superflua la charla de Polonio
> exacto sobre el Príncipe *(Though this be madness there is method in it)*.
>
> (151)
>
> [Asked about the nature of the poem, Laforgue replied:
> *"Ni mon ni mon art, Monsieur."*
> Which figures,
> just as his sarcasms about the moonlight
> makes superfluous precise Polonius's lecture
> about the Prince *(Though this be madness there is method in it)*.]

These seven lines cut across national and linguistic barriers to demonstrate how various systems of meaning are connected by their common roots in the Western tradition of thought. However, by not presenting these works in their proper chronological order, the speaker sets himself in opposition to one of the accepted rules of the modern world: that is, that ideas move in a progression until a definitive resolution is found. Here we see that none of the works or commentaries proves the others wrong: although they may undermine ("hace superflua") the others' works, they also support them by repeating them and glossing them. They, like *Hamlet*, offer a series of representations that never resolves the questions at hand, though "there is method in it."

The speaker underscores this point later in the poem by glossing his own text in footnotes, a technique that suggests that there is neither a final nor an original word, and by discussing the inherent multiplicity of literature in more explicit terms. Thus his repeated quotation of Bison Ravi (Boris Vian)—"*A mort le pléonasme*"—is ironic, first because he does repeat it, and second, because he tells us that literature is a process of "aventajar la glosa," the continual revision of the same old story. Despite the inherent frustration of this process, however, the tone is not one of despair but of hope. This very pleonasm, the eternal erasing and reinscribing of the word, saves us from the opacity of habit by offering us "una vasta gama" [a vast gamut] with which to eternally recreate our lives. The resistance to closure is a form of freedom, a key to life.

The repetition of Bison Ravi's statement in this poem underscores the importance of pleonasm, for it shows how the same words may acquire a different meaning in a different context. The repetition of lines calling for an end to repetition follows an extended discourse on the value of the continual rewriting of the world. This context, and the repetition itself, undermines the supposed import of the quotation and communicates the opposite of what is apparently intended by the phrase. The phrase also changes subtly for us if we know something about the author cited and the probable context in which he penned these words. Bison Ravi was the "anagrama usual de Boris Vian" [the usual anagram of Boris Vian], as the speaker informs us in a footnote. Vian, a novelist, playwright, musician, opera composer, and engineer, wrote works during the 1930s and 1940s that anticipated the absurdist works of the 1950s and 1960s in their creation of purely linguistic worlds. It is also important to note that he was a radical who, like Carnero and other culturalist writers, abstained from politics, and he was an anarchist. He performed a purely cultural rebellion by buying foreign works, listening to American jazz, and imitating English customs during the German occupation. Citing his work twice and footnoting the source represents a cultural rebellion in itself, a will to resist the dominant culture by quoting subversive texts. This quotation, then, serves as an example of the plurality and significance of pleonasm by showing how context may change meaning and how pleonasm itself (Vian's repetition of jazz, Carnero's repetition of Vian) may constitute a form of cultural rebellion.

The second part of the poem calls for exactly that type of rebellion. Although it appears to simply describe the act of creation, it actually defines that act as one of subversion against the very values that give rise to creation. Because it is constituted of words, the poet tells us, the poem is perfectly suited to the task of showing the instability of language. It is therefore in a key position for undermining the power of rational constructs (science, the concept of progress, philosophy) as well as other absolutist systems based upon language. As the speaker explains,

> El poema procede de la realidad
> por vía de la violencia: realidad viene a ser
> visualizar un caos desde una perspectiva
> que el poeta preside desde el punto de fuga.
> Grandeza del poema, la del héroe trágico;
> un modo de atentar contra el método empírico
> desde su misma entraña, como aquel poseído
> ofendía la ley desde el sometimiento.
>
> (152)

> [The poem proceeds from reality
> by means of violence; reality comes to be
> visualizing a chaos from a perspective
> over which the poet presides from the vanishing point.
> The grandeur of the poem, that of the tragic hero;
> a way of making an attempt against the empirical method
> from within its very heart, as that possessed person
> offended the law from a position of compliance.]

Poetry subverts language from within. And, since language synecdochically represents society,[9] we may conclude that the poet and his work subvert society by exposing the fragility of its rules. By showing their own vulnerability, the poet and the poem reveal that of other authorities, but they avoid annihilation through their seeming conformity to the rules that govern society. This idea is underscored once more by pleonasm, the reworking of old themes in new contexts. The poet is converted into Hamlet, the "héroe trágico" and author of various reenactments of his father's murder. Like Hamlet, the poet cannot rebel openly for fear of losing his own life. Still, he is able to reveal the king's corruption in a play sanctioned by the king. He remains within the system and subverts it by representing its corruption, hoping that his feigned madness will prevent his elimination. "Though this be madness, there is method in it."

The concept of "authority" is further weakened by the speaker's insistence on the importance of the continual reworking of ideas to the very

2 / A Question of Authority: *El sueño de Escipión*

continuation of life. Earlier, he had explicitly linked writing and living ("siendo vivir un modo de escritura" [life being a form of writing]); here he emphasizes that we should never reach a conclusion if we hope to live:

> Poema es una hipótesis sobre el amor escrito
> por el mismo poema, como sabemos todos,
> entre ambos modos de escritura
> no hay corrección posible: como puede observarse
> *no* nos movemos en un círculo
>   para gloria del arte
> y sin embargo evítese
> tal conclusión en práctica:
> la palabra en perjuicio de la tragedia íntima
> lo mismo que su opuesto;
>   ¿*qu'adviendrait-il alors*
> *de cette absence de mystère?*
>
>   (152)

> [Poem is a hypothesis about love written
> by the poem itself, as we all know,
> between both modes of writing
> there is no possible correction: as you can observe
> we do *not* move in a circle,
>   for the glory of art
> and yet avoid
> such a conclusion in practice:
> the word in detriment to the intimate tragedy
> just like its opposite;
>   ¿*qu'adviendrait-il alors*
> *de cette absence de mystère?*]

The quotation of Mallarmé is particularly relevant, because it illustrates the end that the speaker hopes to avoid, the elimination of life's mystery. More important, however, it serves as yet another example of pleonasm. This reworking of the same questions is essential, and it is more than relevant that with each repetition the answers change. We cannot—and, what is more, we should not—reach a single definitive conclusion.

    This idea is further elaborated in the third part of the poem. We see that the world is infinitely complex and referential, and that, therefore, all of our repeated probings into its meaning are significant.

> Indignaban a Pico
> los pulcros paradigmas de Careggi,
> que *la inteligencia, la vista y el oído*
> *son los únicos medios de gozar la belleza*
> *y existe por lo tanto una triple beldad*
> o que *la belleza de un cuerpo es su simetría*
> *de donde amor no exige más cosa que templanza*
> *y buen gusto.*
>   De ahí
> su bien lograda máxima: *No hay belleza en un dios.*
>
>   (152–53)
>
> [Pico became indignant
> at the tidy paradigms of Careggi,
> that *intelligence, sight and hearing*
> *are the only means of enjoying beauty*
> *and there exists therefore a triple beauty*
> or that *the beauty of a body is its symmetry*
> *from which love asks no more than temperance*
> *and good taste.*
>   From that,
> his well-formed maxim: *There is no beauty in a god.*]

These ideas are too neat: they imply that beauty is symmetrical and easily explained. If that were the case, art would not be necessary, for, once the abstract concepts were diagrammed, the artist's task would be complete. Pico's art was anything but clear; he valued obscurity and symbolism. The speaker likewise asserts that we can never fully represent reality in art, but our repeated attempts to do so add to the picture without completing it.

    By quoting both the concepts of the Careggi school and Pico de Mirandola's response to them, this poem shows the dynamic quality of literature and its empowering impact on its readers. If readers become incensed upon reading a text, they may unravel what they believe to be its intended meaning and reweave the tapestry in a different way. For example, Pico's indignation at the Careggi interpretation of artistic meaning (freely translated by Carnero from a discourse by Cavalcanti in Marsilio Ficino's commentary on Plato) incites him to discourse, for he hopes to correct that error. As a humanist, he must contest that "*No hay belleza en un dios.*" "El sueño de Escipión," in turn, responds to and reworks Pico's (and Careggi's and Laforgue's and Shakespeare's and Boris Vian's and Mallarmé's) texts.

The speaker concludes, appropriately, with pleonasm, repeating his own and Pico's idea:

> Y procediendo por analogía,
> que es el modo de ser de este parágrafo,
> resulta (véase el resto del poema):
> *Et vous et votre art, Monsieur.* No hay belleza en un dios.
>
> [And proceeding by analogy,
> which is the mode of being of this paragraph,
> it turns out (see the rest of the poem):
> *Et vous et votre art, Monsieur.* There is no beauty in a god.]

It is important to note that the italicized text, used throughout the poem to denote the citations of others' texts, is employed here with the speaker's own words, and that Pico's words are not italicized. This technique has two effects. First, it highlights the textuality, hence the provisionality, of this text by showing that it, like the others mentioned, may also be cited. Second, it demonstrates how words may change their meaning when placed in a different context: the second time the speaker repeats, "No hay belleza en un dios," it has become his phrase, expressing from his vantage point his concept of the world and its various representations since and including that of Pico himself. The phrase has a new meaning despite the fact that it uses the same words. The result is to blur the concept of the author and authority by foregrounding citation.

The speaker claims to have proved his point that life and art must come together in a work, "*Et vous et votre art.*" He has cited authorities and argued convincingly in support of this theory, and he confidently suggests that we review those arguments ("véase el resto del poema"). When we do so, however, we do not find a single answer but, rather, a plurality of thought, a "vasta gama" of difference. By placing on the same level texts by authors belonging to vastly different ages (the *dolce stil nuovo* period, Neoplatonism, the baroque, symbolism, postmodernism) and countries (Italy, France, Spain, and England), this poem shows that there is no one truth, that the history of literature and of aesthetics is a history of disagreement, of the failure to reach an absolute conclusion. It is, furthermore, a history of dialogue: Laforgue argued with Shakespeare and was changed by him; Pico disputed the conclusions of the Careggi school and was greatly influenced by them. The speaker in "El sueño de Escipión" has a dialogue with all of the above:

he changes them by placing them in a new context, and we must logically conclude that they have changed him. The speaker has shown us, then, that we never reach one absolute truth, yet we continue to seek it, revising what we consider to be the erroneous perceptions of previous generations. This poem reveals, then, that poetry is a product not only of the poet and his art but also of his circumstances and all that came before and will come after him.[10]

"El sueño de Escipión" is, in this sense, a subversive text. It undermines the power of authority by revealing the contingency of truth through the revision, reworking, repetition, and recontextualization of texts and ideas. It shows that no text may be interpreted as the ultimate authority; none has found or revealed the ultimate truth. If we agree that language, of which poetry is composed, is a synecdochical representation of culture that reflects the structure of society as a whole ("Nueve preguntas"), we may conclude, by extension, that the proclamations of other authorities in society are also only partially true. This realization allows us to resist the often convincing pronouncements of religious, political, and social authorities, even if that resistance takes the apparently apolitical form of listening to the forbidden jazz music during the German occupation, or of reading forbidden texts, like those of Boris Vian himself, during the Franco dictatorship. It does not eliminate those authorities, however, nor does it completely decenter them; it only unmasks the mechanism by which they function.

This play of power—its creation, subversion, and re-creation—is the thread that links the poems of *El sueño de Escipión*, despite their technical and thematic differences. All of the poems explore some aspect of the problematic relationship among the poet, reality, the text, and its readers and thereby demonstrate the poet's provisional control over his readers and even over his own creation. The shorter poems examine one or two threads of this complicated web. The longer poems of the book—"Jardín inglés," "Chagrin d'amour," and "El sueño de Escipión"—allow the poet to demonstrate more fully the fragility of poetic authority through extensive allusions, which reveal that the answers to the continuing questions of life change with the context. They furthermore undermine the concept of absolute truth by unmasking the poet: by revealing the very human motives and insecurities that give rise to poetry, these poems demythologize the godlike creator of texts. Behind the mask of authority, we see a fragile figure with an uncertain grasp on language and truth. Despite this questioning, however, we ultimately accept some aspect of the poet's view of reality. That is, despite the subversion of authority in the texts, the poet still creates a frame through which we interpret reality, and he therefore remains an authoritative figure. Furthermore, despite the subversion of the authority of Western texts, the play among those texts remains our focus throughout the book. *El sueño de Escipión*, then, represents not the destruction of power but the exposure of its mechanism, how it controls surely but not completely: "Pero no sin ficción."

3
Forms of Repetition: *Variaciones y figuras sobre un tema de La Bruyère*

REPETITION in postmodern literature unmasks convention and reveals its mechanism; that is, it reveals the artificiality of social and linguistic constructs, and it shows how their recurrence makes them appear natural. It may also serve to decenter the logocentrism of contemporary Western culture by reincorporating time and process (expressed in the metonymic displacement of closure), as well as memory (assisted by pleonasm, anaphora, rhyme, and meter in traditional poetic forms) into the meaning of the word and the speech-act.[1] Given the philosophical bases of Carnero's poetry, it is not surprising that the repetitive function is constant throughout his work despite the various styles of his books. In *Dibujo de la muerte*, images acquire different connotations as they are repeated in different semantical and syntactical contexts; thus metonymy reveals the contingency of signification even as it weaves new webs of meaning. In *El sueño de Escipión*, the repeated insistence on the artificiality of literary creation, in addition to the pleonastic citing of authors, reveals the mechanism of literary power, the play between writers, reality, words, texts, and readers which creates and decenters author-ity.

In *Variaciones y figuras sobre un tema de La Bruyère* (1974) [Variations and figures on a theme by La Bruyère], the repetitive function is primarily represented in the lexical and semantic recurrences within the poems and in the structure of the book as a whole.[2] The form of the book is essentially closed, following a pattern prescribed in the initial poem, "Discurso del método" (157–58) [Discourse on method]:

> y así concebiremos dos tipos de poema: uno "sintético"
> fundado en la generalidad y el lenguaje que le es propio,

3 / Forms of Repetition: *Variaciones y figuras*

    y que este libro llama "variación"—
otro "analítico" que explicita el detalle y arroja luz
sobre la variación; lo llamamos "figura".

(158)³

[and thus we will conceive two types of poem: one "synthetic"
founded in generality and the language that is appropriate to it,
and which this book calls a "variation"—
another "analytical" which explicates the details and throws light
on the variation; we call it a "figure."]

All of these poems are united by the common reference to a theme by La Bruyère, cited in the initial epigraph—"Tout est dit et l'on vient trop tard"—but their interpretation of that phrase varies. They are also linked by the closed structure of the book, in which the three-poem introduction, including the discourse on method, is followed by the four variations (each consisting of two to three sections), which in turn are followed by the five figures that supposedly throw light on some aspect of the variations. Finally, there is a one-poem epilogue, which closes the book.

    The fixity of this structure is undermined, however, by the figures of repetition—the dialogue between the poems, the recurrence of images and phrases, the repeated variations on the same theme and the negations of logocentrism.[4] Where that tradition posits an ideal unity—between word and object, vision and identity, truth and meaning—this book places a dialectical relationship, an unending flux of affirmation and denial, a *process* of signification. Within the variations we find linguistic, semantic, and structural repetitions, metonymy, and negation, which posit and unravel poetic representations of essences. The figures are much shorter poems that use a single voice or image, semantic repetition, allusion, and negation to explore the relationship between interpretation and representation. Both types of poem discuss explicitly the problem of the poetic representation of reality, and both explore the limitations imposed by logocentrism on poetic discourse (which, in turn, created those very limiting concepts). Those limitations are loosened in part by the repetition of images and structures, and by the use of palinodes, all of which present and deny the identity between word, form, and meaning and repeatedly defer interpretive closure. The explicit relationship between the two forms—the figure "arroja luz sobre la variación"—further prolongs the temporal dimension of interpretation and encourages yet another repetition, the rereading of the variations.

    This dialectic between fixed external forms and internal repetition is characteristic of postmodern poetry. It may be found in both the serial and the procedural poetic forms that Joseph Conte describes in his study of postmodern poetry.[5] According to Conte, both the infinite and finite series are generated by metonymy, by the chance connections between words and concepts, but in the finite series each poem is at once a separate text and part of an internally coherent system. The dynamic progression of the divisions (introduction, variations, figures) in *Variaciones y figuras*—from three poems to four, to five—suggests such a serial continuation. The individual figures and the separate sections within the variations, however, are often more procedural in nature. That is:

> lexical recurrence prevails, the commutation of several words or phrases from one place in the poem to another is the principal structural motive. Each reappearance of a word or phrase summons a reevaluation of the sign and of the form itself. . . . The recurrence of a word or phrase immediately recalls its previous appearance and underscores any shift in meaning or context.[6]

The recurrence in these poems is occasionally semantic as well: the "significance of each stanza remains largely the same, though the words and phrases chosen to express that meaning change."[7] The structural division within each variation serves a similar function: the same "message" is communicated in each section of the variation, although with different images and forms. And, of course, each poem is a variation on the same theme, a semantic repetition in itself. Thus, although the relatively closed form of the book and the poems represents a formal limitation, the repetition and transformation between and within the poems actually highlight the arbitrary nature of such formal constraints, the lack of a "natural" correspondence between form and meaning, and they reincorporate the temporal dimension into interpretation.[8] Even the structure of *Variaciones y figuras*, then, represents a theme (of La Bruyère, of the book, of Carnero's poetry, of Berkeley and Kandinsky, cited in the opening epigraphs): a form (a sign, a poetic structure) itself represents not an essential meaning, but an unending and repetitive process of signification.

These concerns are expressed in "Discurso del método," a poem that, in the process of analyzing poetic signification, demonstrates how formal and linguistic conventions, ossified through their repetition, come to define poetic meaning. The language of this poem is decidedly not poetic in conventional terms, yet its spatial disposition and the opening line declare that it is a poem:

3 / Forms of Repetition: *Variaciones y figuras*

En este poema se evitará dentro de lo posible, teniendo en cuenta
las acreditadas nociones de "irracionalidad" y "espontaneidad"
consideradas propias de esta profesión,
usar o mencionar términos inmediatamente reconocibles
como pertenecientes al repertorio de la Lingüística; si se los usa será:
    a) sujetándose a hacerlo de manera asistemática, lo que se justifica
    en razón de que quien pueda leerlos en su verdadero sentido
    tendrá igualmente presente su contexto;
    b) admitiendo que en su valor operativo para los efectos de este poema
    es fácil que tengan, en la Estética tradicional o en el habla común,
    equivalentes adecuados—
                        de este modo
se evitará la acusación de cientifismo. . . .

                                                        (157)

[In this poem we will avoid as much as possible, taking into account
the accredited notions of "irrationality" and "spontaneity"
considered appropriate to this profession,
using or mentioning terms immediately identifiable
as pertaining to the repertoire of Linguistics; if we use them it will be:
    a) constraining ourselves to using them in an asystematic manner,
        which may be justified
    since whoever reads them in their true sense
    will equally keep in mind their context;
    b) admitting that in their operative value for the effects of this poem
    it is possible that they will have, in traditional Aesthetics or in common
        speech,
    adequate equivalents—
                            in this way
we will avoid the accusation of scientism.]

These lines explicitly address the issue of conventionality: "scientific language" is not considered appropriate for poetry, but "irrational" and "spontaneous" language is. However, the pseudoscientific language of the opening lines violates that convention. This immediate conflict between linguistic form (scientific language) and meaning ("we will not use scientific language") reveals the artificiality of language itself and specifically of "poetic language." It raises a key question: to what extent is "poetic language" defined by consensus (who will do the accusing?) and convention, rather than some essential correspondence between form and meaning? The artificiality of poetic convention is further foregrounded through the structure of the poem:

the use of verses marks this discourse as "poetry," but within that poetic structure we see a more scientific language and form, complete with subpoints. The poem goes on to describe both kinds of discourse as "poetry," since "toda terminología especializada adquiere, por su sentido arcano / y supuestamente preciso, un gran valor poético" (157) [all specialized terminology acquires, for its arcane / and supposedly precise sense, a great poetic value]. Even while explicitly agreeing with the conventional exclusion of "inappropriate" discourse, this poem flaunts that convention by including scientific formulations.

The reification of poetic form and language is further eroded in the following series of dichotomies. "Accepted" poetic discourse itself is divided into two apparently contradictory forms: (1) the symbolic, characterized by the fusion of form and meaning and linked to science by its extreme rationality, and (2) the avant-garde, defined by its chaotic form and its irrational dislocation of form and meaning. This kind of binary opposition is next echoed in the description of the "synthetic" variations and the "analytical" figures of this book, which I cited above. The repetition and modification of a series of dichotomies within the structure of this poem constitute a syntactic repetition, and they have the effect of reducing the stability of each binary opposition by relating their terms metonymically to those in the other oppositions. Thus "scientific discourse" is not limited to science, since it is reflected in symbolism. Scientific language is also described as a form of poetry; so we may surmise that it also contains its share of irrationality and spontaneity. The definition of both discourses has become a reified convention. This poem, by repeating the same dichotomy in different forms, suggests that convention itself is a product of repetition and that repetition may also unmask and erode it. The same is true of the structure: the disposition of the text on the page is a visual sign of closure, but the repetitions within that structure suggest that the form imposes only a temporary restraint upon the process of signification.

The first variation, "Domus áurea," employs more traditionally poetic language and form than "Discurso del método," but once again repetition and negation defer interpretive closure. The poem is divided into three sections, each of which foregrounds a different type of repetition—lexical, semantic, or formal—to develop the same concept. In the first section of the poem, images and phrases that initially seem metaphoric are repeated and transformed, signaling an unending process of defining words, ideas, and figures.

3 / Forms of Repetition: *Variaciones y figuras*

La sordidez es nuestro pan
se inserta entre los cuerpos como un huésped incómodo
y opera en sus volúmenes
la falsación del aire
. . . .
Parodia nuestros gestos a los pies de la cama,
dibuja el garabato de la carne desnuda
en que creemos estar vivos.
. . . .
La sordidez es nuestro pan,
nos provee de odio y en él somos lenguaje
que sin embargo deteriora,
levantamos un muro de palabras
que el odio deteriora; parodiándolo
nos envuelve en palabras como velos.
Envolverse en palabras como velos
para mitificar las figuras del odio
como las estaciones de la risa,
porque el discurso del fracaso,
la lucidez, la fantasmagoría,
son un arte de amar, tienen su método
como lo tiene el uso de la carne
cuando creemos estar vivos,
cuando desdice al odio
con sus fabulaciones, la noche que no dura.
. . . .
La sordidez es nuestro pan,
origen del discurso que llamamos poema,
origen del discurso de la carne
en que creemos estar vivos,
envueltos en palabras como velos.
Odio, carne, poema: palabras como velos.

(161–62)

[Sordidness is our bread,
it inserts itself between bodies like an uncomfortable guest
and performs in their volumes
the falsification of the air
. . . .
It parodies our gestures at the foot of the bed,
it outlines the scrawl of naked flesh

in which we believe to be alive.
. . . .
Sordidness is our bread,
it provides us with hatred and in it we are language
which nonetheless deteriorates,
we raise a wall of words
which reduces itself to hatred,
and the hatred deteriorates; parodying it
wraps us in words like veils.
Wrapping us in words like veils
to mythify the figures of hatred
like the seasons of laughter
because the discourse of failure,
lucidity, phantasmagoria,
are forms of loving, they have their method,
just as the use of the flesh has one
when we believe we are alive
when hatred is unsaid
by the fabulations of the night that does not last.
. . . .
Sordidness is our bread,
origin of the discourse we call the poem,
origin of the discourse of the flesh
in which we believe to be alive,
wrapped in words like veils.
Hatred, flesh, poem: words like veils.]

This poem begins with a metaphorical construction—"La sordidez es nuestro pan"—a formulation that implies fixity, atemporality, and closure. The repetition of that phrase and others in the poem could suggest that solidity as well—"un muro de palabras." However, that same repetition displaces the meaning of these words in both temporal and semantic terms by forcing us to reconsider them later in different contexts. It also reveals that the words are artificial, rather than natural or essential, constructs, since their meaning is a function of repetition. Thus, all of the central images of the poem—hatred, the flesh, the word—seem solid at the beginning of the poem, but their interconnections and their repetition deconstruct the structural walls they build. Sordidness is connected to the flesh through the image of bread, which in Communion becomes the flesh; hatred constructs walls with the words that veil the flesh and build the poem; the flesh and the poem are forms of discourse; all of these deteriorate. These images are also

3 / Forms of Repetition: *Variaciones y figuras*

metonymically related by their contiguity within a stanza, or a sentence, culminating in the final verse, where they appear together: "Odio, carne, poema: palabras como velos." Were it not for the process of the rest of the poem, the words in that last verse might there be taken for metaphor; as it is, those apparently solid words represent a process of signification. The imprecision of the word "como" likewise dislodges the concept of identity and permanence implicit in metaphor.

If lexical recurrence is the primary form of repetition in the first section of "Domus áurea," then semantical recurrence characterizes the second. This section begins with a tentative definition of poetic discourse:

> El discurso poético
> fueran haces de signos surgidos en el aire,
> emanación
> de la presencia pura de volúmenes juntos
> o colores o masas.

(162)

> [Poetic discourse
> would be beams of signs anchored in the air,
> emanation
> of the pure presence of joined volumes
> or colors or masses.]

This half-hearted formulation of a logocentric concept of poetic discourse suggests that one word may be substituted for another: "de la presencia pura de volúmenes juntos / *o* colores *o* masas." This is exactly what we see in the following lines, in which one simile is substituted for another, and all repeat the tenets, tentativeness, and imprecision of the opening lines:

> Lo mismo que la nave
> es ritmo por la doble pulsación de los remos
> donde todo es presencia como el yute o el cáñamo
> o el lino y la madera con sus triples argollas
> y esa presencia es música.
>   Como a un lado del muro
> las significaciones que afligen al poema
> palpitan con su mugre, y más adentro
> no destila el violín más que una forma
> inmóvil en color y al escucharse ausente.
>   Lo mismo que

> la roca
> es una arista dócil a la mano
> tan irreconocible que carece
> de partes, a lo sumo es un color
> extenso, que ante el mar no significa
> y sonoro en las olas que no tienen historia. . . .
>
> (163)

> [The same as the ship
> is rhythm because of the double pulsation of the oars
> where all is presence like the jute or the hemp
> or the linen or the wood with its triple bands
> and that presence is music.
> As on one side of the wall
> the significations that afflict the poem
> palpitate with their grime, and further within,
> the violin does not exude more than a form
> immobile in color and, upon being heard, absent.
> The same as
> the rock
> is an edge that is ductile to the hand
> so unrecognizable that it lacks
> parts, at the most it is a color,
> extensive, which before the sea does not signify
> and resonant in the waves that have no history. . . .]

These definitions assert an essential correspondence—"Lo mismo que"—but they are imprecise in themselves because they are only similes and because they are characterized more by absence and denial than by presence. The fact that they are presented as substitutes for one another—they are all similes that seek to represent poetic discourse—further undermines the "essential" relationship between the image and the referent. That correspondence is additionally blurred by the culminating negation of the final lines of this section:

> no así el poema: viejos estandartes
> llamados a contar siempre la misma hazaña
> intentando la música que los cuerpos omiten
> y enturbian las palabras con su fango:
> no hay palabras ni cuerpos nacidos en el aire.
>
> (163)

3 / Forms of Repetition: *Variaciones y figuras*   85

>   [not thus the poem: old standards
>   called upon to recount always the same deed
>   the music attempting what the bodies omit
>   and the words sully with their mire:
>   there are no words or bodies born in the air.]

Not even the foregoing definitions, with all their imprecision, describe poetic discourse, which is here given as a negation of even that fuzzy essence. The semantic repetition of this section represents poetic meaning as a temporal and pleonastic phenomenon rather than as an ideal and atemporal identification of sign and referent, "signos surgidos en el aire." Finally, this section constitutes, in its entirety, a semantic repetition of the first section, and, as such, it once again defers interpretive closure.

The last section of "Domus áurea" employs a formal repetition—of unrhymed quatrains—and a plethora of negative words and prefixes to further explore the relationship between form and meaning. The connection between this section and the others is apparent from the first line, which contrasts directly with the last line of the previous section, "no hay palabras ni cuerpos nacidos en el aire":

>   Qué hermosura los seres nacidos en el aire
>   no en el aire poblado de las grutas marinas
>   donde rasguean trépanos de algas
>   y amenaza el susurro de las bestias del fondo
>
>   ni el aire batido del estrecho
>   inerme al remolino de las rocas gemelas
>   que recoge la imagen la sombra de las alas
>   pendientes en el cielo y son materia,
>
>   o el aire de las cumbres
>   que inexpugnan los ecos sin orilla
>   y ve la sucesión de sombra y luz;
>   luz y sombra son cambio: son materia.
>
>   (163–64)

>   [How beautiful the beings born in the air
>   not in the air populated by marine grottoes
>   where trepans of algae strum
>   and the whisper of the beasts of the deep threatens

nor the beaten air of the strait
defenseless against the whirlpool of the twin rocks
that retrieves the image of the shadow of the wings
which hang in the sky and are matter,

or the air of the peaks
that unassail the shoreless echoes
and sees the succession of shadow and light;
light and shadow are change: they are matter.]

Whereas the lexical repetition of "son materia" recalls the style of the first section of "Domus áurea," the negation and the semantical repetition (the substitution of images to represent the air) recalls the second. The first lines posit the existence of poetic beings born in the air, but the definition of the air that could conceive such beings becomes a process of elimination—not this one, nor the other—since all is matter, even the word. This process denies logocentrism by repeating the impossibility of a transcendental signified; the several attempts to define the air negatively have the effect of undefining it and of deferring spatial and temporal closure, a process that culminates in the final stanza—"Aire no que no anula la distancia" (164) [Air not that does not nullify distance].

In contrast to the other sections of "Domus áurea," this section focuses more on the unstable connection between a closed poetic structure and meaning. The quatrains and the frame of the first and last lines—"Qué hermosura los seres nacidos en el aire" and "Nacidos en el aire"—imply stability, timelessness, and closure. However, the fluctuation of verse lengths, the lack of rhyme, and the negativity decenter the attempts to define, to close meaning. Even the closure implied by the quatrain is unstable because that stanzaic form is repeated within the frame of the poem, and the frame itself reaches beyond this section to the previous section, as I described. The precariousness of form is even represented in the final quatrain by a structural break in the last verse:

> Aire no que no anula la distancia,
> el sonido, el color y las pirámides
> de luna en que se finge la quietud
> y es materia.
>   Nacidos en el aire.
>
> [Air not that does not nullify distance,
> sound, color and the pyramids

3 / Forms of Repetition: *Variaciones y figuras*

>   of moon in which stillness is feigned
>   and is matter.
> >   Born in the air.]

This break serves to set off the frame mentioned above and to highlight the contrast between what the word and the poem are ("materia") and what they would be ("Nacidos en el aire"). The form of this poem, then, foregrounds the artificiality of form, and, along with the semantic and lexical repetitions, it reincorporates time into the interpretive process by forcing a rereading and, finally, a pause.

In many ways "Domus áurea" is a microcosm of *Variaciones y figuras*. Each section of the poem presents a different form of repetition—lexical, semantic, formal—and each is a semantic repetition of the first, representing a variation on the theme of the linguistic and literary sign. The repetitions within and between the sections demonstrate the temporality and imprecision of meaning and the artificiality of form. They open up the interpretive process by encouraging rereadings, and they are themselves examples of rereadings. The negation within these forms also denies closure; even the closed form of the third section and of the poem as a whole implies the instability of form and closure. In fact, the coexistence of form and images with the negation of them suggests that meaning is not a question of "either/or" but of "either/and."

The other poems in this part of the book are, in turn, variations on the first, and as such they form a closed cyclical structure; but again, the repetitive techniques and negations unravel that closure. The second variation, "Queluz," contrasts the unlimited referents—"no tienen nombre" (166) [they have no name]—to their delimitation by the walls constructed of language, "de la nada" (167) [from nothingness].

>   Porque el mar no termina
> ni es mar ni tiene fin ni existen "donde"
> ni "mar" ni "fin".
>
>   (166)
>
>   [Because the sea neither ends
> nor is it sea nor does it have an end nor exist "where"
> nor "sea" nor "end."]

The use of quotation marks here foregrounds the artificiality of "mar," suggesting that the word already implies a concept or image, as do the other terms of the phrase "el mar no termina." The structure and import of the final verse of this section recall those of the first section of "Domus áurea" ("Odio, carne, poema: palabras como velos"). Here we read, "ola, noche, color: no tienen nombre" (166) [wave, night, color: they have no name]. As in the earlier poem, the repetition of these words reminds us that they are not the referent, but a reification of it (not the signified, but the sign; not a pure metaphorical correspondence, but a petrified metonym). The second half of the line "no tienen nombre" constitutes a lexical repetition within this poem, and foregrounds again the artificiality of the name and its limiting function.

In the second section of "Queluz" we learn that the words and the walls are related to another human emotion—fear rather than the hatred and love of "Domus áurea." Still, the repetition of forms and images from the first variation brings to mind the formulation of the earlier poem and again opens the interpretive possibilities. At the end of this poem, things are named, but that naming is not a correspondence; it occurs only when those things are "ya no reconocibles en su sustancia misma" (168) [no longer recognizable in their very substance]. This naming thus represents the limitation of signification, which is nonetheless undermined by the repetition and negation in the poem and by the intertextuality with the first variation.

"Sotheby's," the third variation, repeats the first variation structurally, exploring the limitations of *logos* by repeatedly comparing it to the process it halts. As in "Domus áurea," this poem has both lexical and semantic repetitions. The former consist primarily of the recurrence of the phrases "descifrar es" [interpretation is] and "no es descifrar" [is not interpretation]; interpretation is thus represented as a repetitive process that can itself be defined repetitively and negatively (by what it is not). That negative points to the difference between the logocentric sign and the referent: the former is eternal and unified, whereas the latter is temporal and plurivalent. This difference is expressed in a series of images that come to constitute semantic recurrence: a stable sign is as unnatural as the shadow of a bird halted in midflight over a flowing river; it is as artificial as the reflection of a bridge on that river; that magical sign becomes artifacts, treasures, bones, housed in a museum, then an ossuary. That sign, the word, does not equal the referent, "la inmersión final de los tonos / que los siete nombres del color envilecen e ignoran" (171) [the final immersion of the tones / that the seven names of color defile and ignore]. Despite the ossification described in the poem, the instability of the definition of "descifrar" and the recurrence of a phrase from the previous poem—"que tiene nombre ahora"—encourage

3 / Forms of Repetition: *Variaciones y figuras*

rereading, reinterpretation, and they thereby reincorporate time and process into the act of deciphering and into the sign itself.

The fourth variation, "Dad limosna a Belisario," discusses further the function of time in the processes of writing and interpretation. The first section of the poem consists of an extended metaphor—that of the poem as a house constructed of signs, which comes to be emptied of life through time. It becomes "una ilusión de vida / coloreada y presente como un Museo de Cera" [an illusion of life / colored and present as a Wax Museum],

> convertido en un brillante simulacro
> el fastuoso fraude en que el tiempo se anula
> si es que el tiempo existió: si es que no es ahora
> real, más que entonces acaso, lo que el tiempo destruye,
> si es que no produce el lenguaje sus propios fantasmas
> que proyectados hacia atrás inventan una realidad posible
> de que ellos serían reflejo, puesto que de la nada
> nada se engendre, y hasta el torpe cadáver que las palabras hilan
> ha de ser hijo de una realidad anterior en el tiempo.
>
> (173)

> [converted into a brilliant simulacrum
> the fatuous fraud that time annihilates
> if in fact that time existed; if it is not now
> real, even more than then, perhaps, that which time destroys,
> if in fact that language does not produce anything but its own phantasms
> which, projected backward, invent a possible reality
> of which they would be a reflection, since nothingness
> nothing engenders, and even the awkward cadaver that words weave
> must be the child of a reality previous in time.]

Again, the lexical repetition and negation ("si es que," "si es que no") defers meaning and closure, despite the explicit denial of the connection between the word, the poem, and time.

The second section of the poem serves as a conclusion to the variations part of the book, summarizing the argument and repeating the central figure, that of the words, which wrapped us in a veil in "Domus áurea" and here "nos envuelven en su manto de plomo, / nos inmovilizan las manos" (174) [wrap us in their cloak of lead, / immobilize our hands]. The conclusion seems to be that those who put too much store in the power of the word as *logos*, as an eternal and fixed form, miss the boat, "la fiesta de los sentidos" [the festival of the senses]. Throughout the variations, this idea has been represented formally, as the stability of the word and structure has been undermined by negation and repetition, which reincorporate time and process into the linguistic and literary sign.

The five figures are much shorter poems, each one dedicated to the presentation of one voice, one perspective, or one facet of linguistic representation. Despite this singularity, they each represent a rereading of the variations, and as such they constitute a semantic repetition that incorporates temporality and memory into the book by encouraging readers to return to the earlier poems and to reconsider them. They also allude to other literary texts and thereby recover some of the lost historical sense of the word and the poem.

"Palabras de Tersites" is a particularly complex example of this process. The speaker of this poem is Thersites, a minor character in the *Iliad*, a work that itself retells history and employs repetitive devices to aid memory. Thersites is a bitter character, and his hatred helps him construct the wall of words ("Domus áurea") that is this poem.

> Esa carcasa ocre es Helena, la gracia de la nuca
> aureolada de cabellos traslúcidos.
> Los que la amaron son inmortales ahí, en la tierra inverniza
> o bien envejecieron con una pierna rota
> dislocada para mendigar unos vasos de vino—
> y yo, el giboso, el patizambo, me acuerdo algunas veces
> de la altivez biliosa de los jefes aqueos
> considerando la pertinencia del combate,
> inspiración segura de algún poema heroico
> cantor de esta campaña y su cuerpo de diosa:
> polvo para quien no la amó, sus versos humo.
>
> Es la decrepitud lo que enciende esta guerra.
>
> (176)

> [That ocher carcass is Helen, the grace of her neck
> adorned with a halo of translucent hair.
> Those who loved her are immortal there, in the wintry land
> or else they aged with a broken leg
> dislocated so they could beg a few glasses of wine—
> and I, the humpback, the bowlegged, remember sometimes
> the bilious haughtiness of the Achaean chiefs
> considering the pertinence of the battle,

3 / Forms of Repetition: *Variaciones y figuras*

   a certain inspiration for some heroic poem
   singing of this campaign and her body like a goddess:
   dust for one who did not love her, his verses smoke.

It is decrepitude that ignites this war.]

This poem demonstrates how words, bodies, love, and hatred disintegrate over time; it thus elaborates upon the theme of the first section of the first variation. The penultimate line illustrates the point of the fourth variation: words that are empty or emptied of experience disintegrate, despite the endurance of the form (of the words, of the poem, of the book). The distance between the referent and its representation is evoked by allusion: this Thersites is separated temporally from the character from the *Iliad*, who is separated by the word and the literary form from the historical person he represents. This separation between poem and referent is exacerbated in this case by the fact that Homer's experience of the Trojan War was purely linguistic; he did not witness the events he transcribed. The reference to the *Iliad* also brings to mind the historical importance of repetition: repetitive devices are themselves historical in the sense that they aid memory and prolong the literary experience. The orality of the epic tale also implies the temporal dimension of the speech-act, which is eliminated when the word becomes *logos*. The *Iliad* is historical and repetitive in another sense as well; it spawned countless literary repetitions (including this poem) and served as a model for countless other epic tales: it is one of the "viejos estandartes / llamados a contar siempre la misma hazaña." The *Iliad* is a historical document in the sense that it is repetition and illusion, "produce el lenguaje sus propios fantasmas / que proyectados hacia atrás inventan una realidad posible / de que ellos serían reflejo" ("Dad limosna a Belisario").

"Mira el breve minuto de la rosa" refers to one of the most often repeated images in the history of the lyric. The rose is a repetition, and in fact, upon reading this rose poem in the context of this book, several others come to mind, most significantly Jorge Luis Borges's "Una rosa y Milton," which connects metonymically to "Palabras de Tersites" through the recreation of the poetic act of a blind poet (or two); and to "Mira" in the use of the rose to explore the problematic relationship between the linguistic sign and the referent. One might also think of Pedro Salinas's "¿Por qué tienes nombre, tú?," which explores the same problem without a rose. This intertextuality reveals both the stultifying and creative potential of repetition, which is the explicit theme of the poem:

Mira el breve minuto de la rosa.
Antes de haberla visto sabías ya su nombre
y ya los batintines de tu léxico
aturdían tus ojos—luego, al salir al aire, fuiste inmune
a lo que no animara en tu memoria
la falsa herida en que las cuatro letras
omiten esa mancha de color: la rosa tiembla, es tacto.
Si llegaste a advertir lo que no tiene nombre,
regresas luego a dárselo, en él ver: un tallo mondo, nada;
cuando otra se repite y nace pura
careces de más vida, tus ojos no padecen agresión de la luz,
sólo una vez son nuevos.

(179)

Observe the brief moment of the rose.
Before having seen it you already knew its name
and already the gongs of your lexicon
dazed your eyes—later, upon going out into the air, you were immune
to whatever did not awaken in your memory
the false wound in which the four letters
omitted that stain of color: the rose trembles, it is touch.
If you came to notice that which had no name,
you returned later to give it one, to see in it: a pure stalk, nothing;
when another is repeated and born pure
you lack more life, your eyes do not suffer the aggression of light,
only once are they new.

The first line of this poem demonstrates what the rest of the poem explains, for after reading that line the reader already has preconceptions about the poem's content. It is very hard to say something new about the rose—this poem is one repetition in a very long series—for that reason, it is the ideal poetic sign to represent the petrification of the meaning of poetic signs. This sign has come to be constituted by its name—its form is r-o-s-e. It is eternal, permanently sealed off from experience, so we do not have even Borges's plurivalence. Even the closure of linguistic form, however, may be loosened by a more historical process, a rereading of the rose through those other roses and in the context of the other images, forms, and recurrences of *Variaciones y figuras sobre un tema de La Bruyére*.

The forms of repetition in *Variaciones y figuras sobre un tema de La Bruyére* give readers a different sense of poetic experience, one that does not reside in the perfect image or form but in the process of change and reinterpreta-

3 / Forms of Repetition: *Variaciones y figuras*

tion within the limits of image and form. This expansion of the sign beyond its form recalls the metonymic and allusive webs of *Dibujo de la muerte* and the pleonasm of *El sueño de Escipión*; both of those books suggest that the sign is plurivalent, temporal, and unstable. Here, the closed structure of the book, the poem, and the image is revealed as the reification of a historical interpretive process, which lexical, semantic, and formal recurrence reveals and reproduces. That is the function of poetry, according to the epilogue entitled "L'enigme de l'heure": to thaw frozen words, to make them signify anew. The language of this final poem harks back to "Discurso del método" and thus serves to structurally close the book. But its theme is repetition, which both limits the word and gives it power. I conclude this rereading of *Variaciones y figuras sobre un tema de La Bruyére, Dibujo de la muerte* and *El sueño de Escipión* with the conclusion to *Variaciones y figuras sobre un tema de La Bruyére*, namely, "L'enigme de l'heure," and the enigma of poetry and the word, of repetition, time, and emotion, repeated here:

> Considera el posible objeto del poema: lo intratable
> por otras formas de saber, un lenguaje llamado
> a la función de emocionar, por mucho que Girondo
> propugnara para la poesía una ley seca.
> Conmover con una palabra mencionada mil veces,
> definida por repetición cuando es oscura,
> que cautiva a la sensibilidad por su monodia,
> y se hace evidente a la razón: en los Libros Proféticos.
> Su gravidez no hacia el significado sino hacia el signo mismo;
> y como el signo, traidor por excelencia, ha de crear su propia carne
> puesto que la nuestra es un mal mensajero,
> hazlo crecer por redundancia, y su presencia repetida
> nos convenza de que sí existe algo tras él: menciona, crea.
>
> El poema es un complejo artesanado, un gran reloj de cuco;
> conocemos su engranaje y cómo da la hora
> que es, con todo, un enigma: también nos duele confesar
> una secreta admiración por Donizetti.
>
> (181)

> [Consider the possible object of the poem: what is intractable
> through other forms of knowing, a language called
> to the function of emotionally moving, however much Girondo
> might advocate for poetry a dry law.
> To move with a word mentioned a thousand times,

defined by repetition when it is obscure,
which captivates sensibility with its monody
and becomes evident to reason: in the Prophetic Books.
Its gravity not toward the signified but toward the sign itself;
and like the sign, traitor par excellence, it must create its own flesh
since ours is a poor messenger,
make it grow through redundancy, and let its repeated presence
convince us that something does exist behind it: mention, create.

The poem is a complex artifice, a great cuckoo clock;
we are familiar with its gears and how it strikes the hour
which is, in the end, an enigma: it also pains us to confess
a secret admiration for Donizetti.]

4
Critical Paranoia:
El azar objetivo

IN an essay entitled "El juego lúgubre: La aportación de Salvador Dalí al pensamiento superrealista" [The gloomy game: Salvador Dalí's contribution to surrealist thought], Guillermo Carnero studies the surrealist artist's paranoiac-critical method, or the rational ordering of a paranoid vision, which, according to Carnero, accomplished the goals of surrealism better than the pure irrationality practiced by some of Dalí's French counterparts.[1] The essay begins with an introductory section in which Carnero criticizes the mental laziness of his compatriots and explains his own motivations and methods before embarking on a description of the tenets of surrealism and Dalí's relationship to the movement. Carnero begins his critical argument by listing the three goals of surrealism—"una triple revolución en tres ámbitos cuya reconstrucción solidaria se considera imprescindible: literatura, moral y política" (J, 138) [a triple revolution in three areas whose solidary reconstruction they considered essential: literature, morals, and politics]. He goes on to describe the three props of this triple revolution: "la Alucinación Voluntaria, el Humor Objetivo y el Azar Objetivo" (J, 139) [voluntary hallucination, objective humor, and objective chance]. The first of these is purely irrational, consisting of the free flow of ideas beyond the limitations of "la moral, la lógica, la tradición literaria y los valores estéticos mostrencos" (J, 139) [morality, logic, literary tradition, and dull aesthetic values]. The second, "objective humor," undermines both external and internal hierarchies: "equivale a la acreencia absoluta en la verdad ontológica de cualquier contenido mental que parezca absurdo, inmoral o improcedente, a la vez que a la descreencia en lo lógico, moral y procedente; mundo al revés" (J, 140) [it is equal to the absolute unbelief in the ontological truth of whatever mental content seems absurd, immoral, or inadmissible, at the same time as the disbelief in what is logical, moral, and admissible; the world upside down]. "Objective chance" represents the final step the surrealist artist must take to realize his triple goal: the tripartite transcendence of the limitations of the "false reality" imposed by cultural paradigms.

According to Carnero, Dalí reaches this state through his paranoiac-critical method. The paranoia allows Dalí to see and represent reality from a position outside of cultural paradigms, but the critical aspect of his program imposes an ordering system upon that paranoid vision. The result is a work that is "*formalmente* lógico (en cuanto responde a un mecanismo deductivo) aunque *ontológicamente* ilógico según la noción de verdad propia de la conciencia superficial" (J, 151) [*formally* logical (to the degree to which it corresponds to a deductive mechanism) although *ontologically* illogical, according to the notion of truth characteristic of superficial consciousness]. The technique, Carnero tells us, has as its goal the discovery of a deep or true meaning that is beyond the reaches of conventional paradigms and beyond irrationality itself. It even surpasses the efforts of the French surrealists, because it resists their communist politics, which had evolved into a kind of dogma from the time of the second manifesto (J, 159). The paranoiac-critical method resists all rational totalizing systems (in part because it creates its own irrational system), and it leads to an epiphany in the realm of *el azar objetivo*.

Readers of Carnero's fourth book of poetry, *El azar objetivo* (1975), may well speculate about the connections between Dalí's aesthetics, Carnero's critical essay, and these poems. One clue may be found at the beginning of the essay, where Carnero laments the recent popularity of Dalí's art and states that his purpose as a critic is to restore its historical dimension and thereby counteract the *cosificación* [reification] implicit in the bourgeois appropriation of the avant-garde.

> El intelectual o el artista están condenados en España a convertirse en cosa. Esa cosificación produce gran alivio en un cuerpo social dominado por la inercia y la abulia e incapaz de destinar sus exiguas energías mentales a actividades de atención, pensamiento y respuesta: porque, en efecto, una *cosa* puede verse privada de significado social y, por tanto, reducida a mera existencia material e inerte o, al contrario, ser investida de ese significado y entrar automáticamente en el circuito que le franquea su valor de cambio. ... Como Salvador Dalí lleva actualmente camino de convertirse en momia lucrativa, no estará de más intentar descosificarlo, aunque ello no sea más que un murmullo del bosque ahogado por la gran zaragata subastadora que se está preparando concienzudamente. (J, 134–35)

4 / Critical Paranoia: *El azar objetivo*

[The intellectual and the artist are condemned in Spain to become things. This reification produces a great relief in a social body dominated by inertia and abulia and incapable of directing its meager mental energies toward activities requiring attention, thought, and response: because, in effect, a *thing* can be seen as void of social significance and, as a result, reduced to a mere inert and material existence or, on the other hand, it may be invested with such significance and enter automatically into the circuit that stamps it with its exchange value. . . . Since Salvador Dalí is in the process of being converted into a lucrative mummy, it is not inappropriate that I attempt to de-reify him, even though it will be no more than a murmur from the forest muffled by the great auction-block brawl that is being painstakingly prepared.]

The vehemence as well as the poetic quality of these lines (their rhythm and use of imagery) reveals the deep emotion of their author, who is distressed to think that the mental inertia of his compatriots condemns vital creations either to oblivion or to the auction block.[2] The desire to protect and restore the life of artistic and intellectual works also implies the emotional investment of the author—who is himself an artist and intellectual—in his argument; he may also wish to save *his* works from oblivion or "cosificación."

In the concluding lines to the introductory section of his essay, Carnero describes his motives, as well as the method and style he will employ in the study, in the most rational language and form imaginable:

Me propongo estudiar en estas páginas la vinculación de Dalí al Superrealismo y las reservas críticas al mismo, traducidas en una aportación fundamental, el método paranoico-crítico; y desde éste explicar la adhesión de Dalí, sólo en apariencia contradictoria, a manifestaciones clásicas y figurativas dentro de la historia del arte, así como las peculiares declaraciones que, fuera del contexto que les es propio, han podido ser interpretadas como síntomas de conservadurismo político o incluso de filofascismo. Me atendré a la letra de los textos, evitando cualquier interpretación que los exceda, y procuraré formular esa interpretación del modo más racional posible, ya que nunca he entendido que pueda un crítico sentirse autorizado a expresarse irracional o nebulosamente, aun cuando trate de fenómenos irracionales, y sobre todo en dicho caso. (J, 137–38)

[I propose to study in these pages Dalí's link to surrealism and his critical reservations about it, translated into a fundamental contribution, the paranoiac-critical method; and from this vantage point explain Dalí's adherence, contradictory only in appearance, to critical and figurative manifestations in the history of art, as well as those peculiar statements that, outside of their proper context, have been open to the interpretation that they are symptoms of political conservatism or even philofascism. I will mind the letter of the texts, avoiding whatever interpretation might exceed them, and I will attempt to formulate that interpretation in the most rational form possible, since it has never been my understanding that a critic may feel himself authorized to express himself irrationally or nebulously, even when dealing with irrational phenomena, and especially in this case.]

The desire to explain, in their intellectual context, those elements of Dalí's work that have been used to label him as a political conservative suggests a further link between Carnero's work and that of Dalí. Is it merely coincidental that Carnero and the other *novísimos* have been unfairly accused of conservatism for their refusal to conform to a specific model of political engagement? The author's personal motives, coupled with the description of Dalí's paranoiac-critical aesthetics, suggest the irrationality (or subjectivity) of even the perfectly logical critical techniques and rigorous scholarship of Carnero's study.

This sensation is even stronger if we consider that the language of this passage clearly recalls the poem "Discurso del método" from *Variaciones*; this intertextuality may invite readers to question the author's separation of rational and irrational language in this essay, since they were explicitly and formally connected in the poem: "toda terminología especializada adquiere, por su sentido arcano / y supuestamente preciso, un gran valor poético" (157) [all specialized terminology acquires, for its arcane and supposedly / precise sense, a great poetic value]. We could ask, why is rational language permissible in a poetic text but irrational language forbidden in a critical one? *Who* does not authorize its use here? *Why* must the critic obey these rules? And why *especially in this case*? Doesn't the paranoiac-critical method itself postulate a deep connection between irrationality and rationality? The foregrounding of the formal rationality of this essay, the links between Dalí and Carnero, and the explanation of the paranoiac-critical method (formal logic, ontological illogic) undermine the ontological logic of the critical essay and the authority of the rules that shape it. The fact that Carnero scrupulously follows those rules here—*especially in this case*—suggests that criticism is itself a kind of paranoid discourse, with its own arbitrary rules, and that the critic Guillermo Carnero is well aware of this contingency.[3]

This type of critical, linguistic, and paradigmatic double bind is represented poetically in *El azar objetivo*. I write "poetically," but the title of the book and the epigraph from Nietzsche immediately bring to mind the instability of the distinction between rational and poetic discourse. Another of the epigraphs, this one from Wittgenstein, suggests why Carnero's vision is, in one sense, even more paranoid than Dalí's. If he hopes to reach the epiphany afforded by *el azar objetivo*, he must create a system, "*formalmente lógico . . . aunque ontológicamente ilógico*," using a medium that itself possesses those attributes: language has a formal logic (grammar) but an ontological irrationality, since words do not correspond to their referents, but rather constitute them. One more distinction may be made between Dalí's poetics and Carnero's: Dalí considers his paranoid vision to be independent of cultural paradigms because it is internal, derived from the subconscious. Carnero, as we have seen, has much less confidence in the independence and integrity of the self. Thus, although both Carnero and Dalí rail against the limitations of bourgeois culture, Carnero's awareness of the contingency of language, and of his own compromised position, generates an endless *mise en abîme* rather than an epiphany, unless the epiphany of this book is the realization that even rebellion is determined by the limits of the system—"como aquel poseído / ofendía la ley desde el sometimiento" (152). In the same way, *El azar objetivo* is framed by Dalí's poetics and Carnero's own critical analysis of them, as well as by Nietzsche and Wittgenstein, themselves framed by Plato (the third epigraph).

Like "El juego lúgubre," *El azar objetivo* foregrounds the ontological illogic of rational discourse by systematically employing some of its formal features in conjunction with irrational poetic images.[4] Thus, the structure of the book as a whole—introduction, body, conclusion—and the language and structure of some of the poems recall the critical essay, but the development of the thesis is largely irrational, incorporating chance elements that upset the balance. The first poem, "Museo de historia natural" (185) [Museum of Natural History], exactly parallels the introduction to "El juego lúgubre" in that it discusses the reification of vital objects by a thoughtless society; it differs in that it poetically, or "irrationally" (see again "Discurso del método"), transforms the artistic objects of the essay into lifeless animal forms displayed in the Museum of Natural History. Their reified forms are "safe" representations of the concept of their power—"gritan terror de estopa, agonía en cartón, violencia plana" [they scream burlap terror, cardboard agony, flat violence]. The motionless, stuffed animals meticulously poised in the exhibits (or interpretations) in the museum have become only "animales simbólicos," but, as in the case of the critical essay, the function of memory and imagination upon them may bring them back to life and make their power real again:

Agazapados tras una puerta distante,
cuando la empuja el simulacro vuelve
a componer su coreografía;
y un día han de invadir los bulevares
de la ciudad desierta, amenazando
la arquitectura fácil del triunfo
y el gesto de la mano que acaricia
la mansedumbre impávida de animales pacíficos.

(185)

[Crouched behind a distant door,
when pushed the simulacrum once again
composes their choreography;
and one day they are destined to invade the boulevards
of the deserted city, threatening
the facile architecture of triumph
and the gesture of the hand that strokes
the dauntless tameness of peaceful animals.]

This poem is clearly linked to the introduction of "El juego lúgubre." The difference lies in the poetic revenge, which is largely repressed in the essay but which is loosed at the end of this poem and in later poems in this book. The reified (physical, artistic, linguistic) forms that were arranged to constitute systems of meaning threaten to literally come to life here and physically destroy those systems and the people who construct them.

The second poem in the book, "La busca de la certeza" (186–87) [The search for certainty], is a humorous send-up of criticism and Western metaphysics, which are here likened to the analysis of one's own excrement, an image that recalls both Nietzsche and Dalí. The humor in this poem is derived primarily from the juxtaposition of the high linguistic register and analytical procedure with the baseness of the material analyzed. Readers are invited to laugh with the poet, for we are all aware of this disjuncture, whereas the subject of the poem is not. This same subject, who appears in the following poems as well, represents the people who do not question the premises of the systems that constitute and generate meanings, but rather use them thoughtlessly to tame reality. In this poem he is doubly exposed, as we observe first his evacuation (at one point he is even inverted so that we may consider the resultant shape of his excrement) and then his attempt to fit the evacuative experience and its product into his metaphysical system.

4 / Critical Paranoia: *El azar objetivo*

> No por esa
> emanación—por así llamarla—modifica
> él su concepto de providencia, mas la admite
> como necesariamente prevista en un orden concluso.
> (186)

> [Not for this
> emanation—so to call it—does he modify
> his concept of providence, rather he admits it
> as necessarily foreseen in a conclusive order.]

These lines comically deflate the notion of cause and effect and a priori knowledge, since the effect is "prevista" only after it appears. (One may think here of Nietzsche's criticism of Kant in *Beyond Good and Evil*.) They also suggest that language often disguises the material it describes: "emanación" is a polite word for this material, and it is polite precisely because of its distance from the odor, texture, and material origin of its referent.

In a particularly graphic image, the poem goes on to reincorporate the physical reality into that substance, likening Western metaphysics and cultural values to a gradually-hardening dunghill, where the subject of the poem leaves his most recent contribution. The subject does not leave it behind, however, but rather applies himself to renewed alimentary efforts so that he may continue to produce similarly substantial forms. Digestion and its by-product have come to constitute, in his mind, an "orden concluso del que espera / felicidad, honor, sabiduría" (187) [conclusive order from which he expects / happiness, honor, wisdom]. This description, coupled with the humor of the poem, undercuts the seriousness and transcendent claims of Western cultural paradigms by showing that a priori postulates, and the metaphysical systems that are constructed from them, are derived a posteriori from the most material of origins.

"La meditación de la pecera" (188–89) [Meditation on the fishbowl] explains more seriously why transcendence is impossible—our language and our physical circumstances determine the limits of our understanding—but, once again, rational language is utilized to represent irrationality, in this case, the irrationality of rationality itself. This poem develops the image of the fishbowl as a metaphor for the limits of human perception. Based upon that image, the poem analyzes point by point the reasons why rationality is impossible: (1) the perfect roundness of the fishbowl precludes the differentiation of one point of view from an infinite number of others; (2) the transparency of the glass prevents us from determining trajectories and distances; (3) the movement of the three fish is random.[5] Even the structure and imagery of this poem form a kind of fishbowl in that its central image (why that image and not another?) and its form (why three points and why three fish?) determine the shape of the argument.

It would only take one note of discord to destroy that harmonious system, and we find that note in the images in the middle of the poem:

> El contemplarla fijamente le induce aún a mayor confusión
> pues le revela una agresividad en
> la materia indócil, tan manejable y breve;
> como aquel protomártir armenio murió luego de la desollación, inútil
> en quebrantar su ánimo, de una simple aspersión de perfume
> mientras una blanquísima esclava desnuda tañía con palillos de jade
> vasos, musicales por estar llenos de agua:
>
> incoherencia.
>
> (188)
>
> [Contemplating it fixedly induces in him even more confusion
> since it reveals to him an aggressiveness in
> the indocile material, so manageable and brief;
> as that Armenian protomartyr died after the skinning, useless
> in breaking his will, from a simple aspersion of perfume
> while the fairest naked slave woman played with jade drumsticks
> on glasses, musical because full of water:
>
> incoherence.]

This digression from the neat and pure fishbowl image is sufficient to reveal its limitations, for it hints at the vast experience and mystery that it cannot contain, the irrational elements that are suppressed in rational ordering systems because they have the potential to destroy their forms and result in incoherence.

Following this digression, the inaccuracy of exact images and language is next expressed as a mathematical figure, a statistic, which epitomizes the precise measurement of a mere possibility, an exact number that is open to interpretation and that measures what does not actually exist. This contradiction is represented linguistically here with extremely precise mathematical language interrupted by a variety of asides and qualifications, and set off by various forms of punctuation (parentheses, brackets, dashes, commas) that break up the sense of the argument and mark its conceptual lacunae.

> Pues si concentra su atención en uno solo
> pensando aislar así los tres problemas a efectos de análisis
> (y signifique esto que son tres los ágiles peces)
> para, una vez delimitada cada trayectoria [su curva
> en un espacio de tres dimensiones (que la esfericidad
> le impide proyectar dichas trayectorias sobre un plano
> como posibilitaría con sus aristas un acuario corriente)]
> con sus variantes codificadas, y a ser posible
> dividida en un breve repertorio de movimientos básicos
> en seriación consigo mismos y con otros
> mediante un número fijo de leyes combinatorias precisas
> con su margen de error asimismo acotable—
> para recomponer entonces, digo, la realidad del fenómeno
> que como un todo no es inmediatamente accesible,
> advierte entonces que, puesto que la entera realidad que se le alcanza
> la constituye el ámbito de la pecera,
> no cabe más referencia para la trayectoria de uno
> que suponer fijo a alguno de los otros.
>
> (189)

> [But if he concentrates his attention on only one,
> thinking to isolate in that way the three problems to effects of analysis
> (and this would mean that there are three agile fish)
> in order to, once each trajectory is fixed [its curve
> in a three-dimensional space (and the sphericity
> hinders him from projecting said trajectories upon a plane
> as a regular aquarium, with its angles, might allow)]
> with its codified variables, and if possible
> divided in a brief repertory of basic movements
> in serialization with themselves and others
> through a fixed number of precise combinatory laws
> with a margin of error likewise measurable—
> in order to recompose, then, as I was saying, the reality of the phenomenon
> which, as a whole, is not immediately accessible,
> he observes then that, given that the whole of reality that is accessible to him
> is constituted by the circumference of the fishbowl,
> he is not left with any other reference point for the trajectory of each
> than to assume that one of the others is fixed.]

The argument is circular, like the fishbowl and the problem it represents. Like the subject of the poem, we start to get lost when the parentheses begin: thus, the confusion that the circularity generates appears linguistically in the ungrammaticality of these lines.

The poem ends on a comic note, though it is that "carcajada metafísica" [metaphysical guffaw] of "objective humor" (J, 141), imbued with a sense of tragedy:

> El problema se muerde la cola
> pero ninguno de los peces lo hace (lo cual o los inmovilizaría
> o los haría girar sobre un eje, lo que es equivalente)
> así que contempla perplejo su indefensión ante el cristal,
> que por falta de centro no termina.
>
> (189)

> [The problem bites its own tail
> but none of the fish does (which would either immobilize them
> or make them spin on an axis, which is the same thing)
> thus he contemplates perplexed his defenselessness before the crystal,
> which for lack of a center does not end.]

The poem, not surprisingly, is also circular and infinite, returning to the unresolved fishbowl image, which contains the mystery of the Armenian protomartyr. The image, the logical argument, the statistical measurement, grammar, and the poem fail to resolve what cannot be resolved, the limitations of understanding, perception and description. The logical structure of the argument does not alter its ontological illogic.

Logically, this central concept—the irresoluble irrationality of rational constructs—is the explicit focus of the central poem (number four of seven), "Elogio de la dialéctica a la manera de Magritte" (191–92) [In praise of dialectics in the style of Magritte]. The painting to which this poem alludes, *In Praise of Dialectics*, serves as an example of the "pecera" of the previous poem. In the painting, the corner window of a building opens inward to reveal the exterior of another building within. Immediately, the definition of "interior" and "exterior" becomes problematic. Obviously, in order to define the spaces of the painting, one term must be held still: if the "exterior" is defined as that which is outside the building, then the windows and doors that are visible through the window must be defined as "interior," although they represent an image that we associate with the exterior of a building. At best, they are part of the exterior of the interior building. However, if "exterior" is defined as a kind of surface, then those same windows and doors are exterior. What is more, the exterior wall to which the framing window belongs is not visible in the painting, but it is symbolically represented by what we see through the window, that is, inside the building. By extension, we could conclude that the exterior of the exterior building is interior in that it is symbolically contained within another space. The definition of the "interior" provides similar difficulties, since there is an "implied interior" beyond the exterior-wall-inside-the window. Similar difficulties in defining the outside and the inside, along with their physical contiguity, create metonymic connections between the apparently opposite spatial concepts, complicating the facile distinction between them. The concepts of "interior" and "exterior" are thereby revealed as arbitrary, provisional, and infinitely regressive ("el problema se muerde la cola"). Furthermore, if we consider that "interior" and "exterior" are three-dimensional spaces, but the painting that represents them is two-dimensional, we become even more aware of the contingency of our concept of space.

Carnero's poem is an explication and a representation of Magritte's painting, and, further, a critique of interpretations that seek to impose definitive order and meaning on art or reality. Here, the conceptual bind is represented by the crucial play on two words, "se anudan" [join together] and "se anulan" [nullify themselves], opposites that are linguistically nearly identical, separated by a single phoneme.[6] Like "interior" and "exterior," they are conceptually counterposed but metonymically linked, and their apparent binarism reveals itself as a mere construct as they come to be substituted for one another in this poem. The distinction between them thus comes to be more a question of chance—*d* or *l?* flip a coin! Yet an entire philosophical system may be built upon the results: *d,* it's Plato and his heirs, *l,* it's Nietzsche and his. This dialectic plays itself out in Carnero's poem through an analysis of how the subject interprets objects found together: Are they necessarily related, or does their connection owe to chance and our interpretive efforts? That is, are they nullified, do they cancel each other out?

> Allí los alinea sin intención aparente
> (atento tan sólo a los límites de tan reducido espacio
> como en espera de que manifiesten ellos mismos, rescatados del caos,
> algún criterio por que distribuirlos en grupos homogéneos)
> quien ha dejado de confiar en que cada uno dicte
> una sucesividad no en busca de sentido

cuanto demostración de que le es accesible
la evidencia del germen en que acaso se anudan.
Más allá de su presencia visible se ¿anudan?
por leyes que no son las ingenuas: contigüidad
en el tiempo, semejanza, generación—
de las que se intuye completamente ignaro; y la obsesión clasificatoria
podría ser allí tanto efecto como causa
por omitir el entusiasmo, pero al cabo es segura.

(190)

[He aligns them there without an apparent intention
(attentive only to the limits of such a small space
as if waiting that they themselves manifest, rescued from chaos,
some criterion with which to distribute them in homogeneous groups)
he who has ceased to believe that each one dictates
successiveness not in search of meaning
as much as a demonstration that there is accessible to him
the evidence of the origin in which, perhaps, they unite.
Beyond their visible presence they unite?
for reasons that aren't the ingenuous ones: contiguity
in time, similarity, generation—
from which one may intuit with complete ignorance; and the obsession
    with classification
could be the effect there as easily as the cause
since it omits enthusiasm, but it is in the end certain.][7]

These lines immediately place the concept of rational order into doubt, questioning from the start the relationship between the objects represented. Their presence signals difference, so the subject seeks an explanation "más allá de su presencia visible." They meet, perhaps—"acaso se anudan"—in a transcendent realm, or do they ("se ¿anudan?")? The sense of doubt predominates; even if there is order, it seems random rather than rational, and changeable rather than static, like the fish in the fishbowl. For that reason, perhaps, the subject searches for a safe order, which nonetheless "podría ser tanto efecto como causa." It is also in movement and in doubt, although, for now, it is secure, reassuring, and safe.

The process of classification immediately becomes problematic as well, as the subject sorts the objects before him and invents categories for them in an effort to codify or "cosify" them. After seven lines, the central doubt appears, tied to the question of presence:

4 / Critical Paranoia: *El azar objetivo*

cómo una búsqueda
fundada en la improvisación de categorías distintivas
(a base de rasgos presentes) de lo que no es presente?
y precisamente de lo que los hace no distintos
sino iguales, algo que no es tangible aunque sí lo contengan
de algún modo—
                que una vez obtenido
los excluye en cuanto los priva de función
puesto que por ninguna manipulación previsible conducen
al término de que son único indicio.

(190–91)

[how to conduct a search
founded upon the improvisation of distinctive categories
(based on present features) of that which is not present?
and precisely of what makes them not different
but equal, something that is not tangible even if they do contain it somehow—
                that once obtained
excludes them as it deprives them of function
since by no foreseeable manipulation do they lead
to the end of which they are the only indication.]

The subject is tying himself in knots trying to sort the objects, with their palpable and visual differences, according to a similarity that is neither visible nor palpable: it is not present. If he focuses on the objects themselves, he sees difference; but if he imagines a similarity, he no longer sees the objects, with their obvious differences. These differences destroy any possible transcendent meaning the objects could have; thus, ironically, the presence of the diverse objects destroys the presence of their common meaning. Difference transforms "se anudan" into "se anulan":

Entonces considera la extensión de su manta
con los objetos que por su presencia visible se anulan
pues no se allana en ella la diversidad y queda en superficie
antes bien, replanteando de ese modo
no sólo la diversidad misma, de suya caprichosa
cuanto producto de la voluntad del que alinea,
sino el intento mismo de diversificar y arrojar luz así.

(191)

> [Then he considers the extension of his blanket
> with the objects that, because of their visible presence, cancel each
>   other out
> since diversity does not yield to it and remains on the surface
> rather, restating in that way
> not only diversity itself, which is in itself capricious
> as a product of the will of the one who aligns,
> but the very attempt to diversify and shed light that way.]

Even "diversity" is an abstraction; the diversity of the objects remains on the surface and resists "deep" meaning. The problem is like that in Magritte's painting. What is similarity and what is difference? What is presence and what is absence? What is superficial and what is profound or transcendent? The concepts cannot be definitively grasped:

> Y bien, cuando los contempla fijamente le huyen,
> y en el brillo lustroso con que aquel ir y venir los decora
> además de afirmarse, aún provocan a risa
> pero no a él, pues es risa de las superficies rotundas
> dando fe del volumen que a pesar suyo exhiben;
> por más que el procedimiento se le revele inane
> persiste, que aunque estéril es al cabo seguro.
>
> (189)

> [And so, when he contemplates them fixedly they escape him,
> and in the lustrous shine with which that coming and going adorns
>   them
> in addition to affirming themselves, they still provoke laughter
> but not from him, since it is the laughter of rounded surfaces
> testifying to the volume that they exhibit despite themselves;
> as much as the procedure reveals its inanity to him
> he persists, since, although sterile, it is in the end certain.]

As in Magritte's painting, the limitations of the artistic medium add further complexity to the dialectic of this poem. Magritte's subject was space, but the three-dimensional concepts of exterior and interior played out their relationship on a two-dimensional canvas, where neither "really" exists. Carnero's focus is on presence, but his objects' physical presence and their meaning appear and disappear only in words, where neither "really" exists. The linguistic sign marks the presence and the absence of the objects and their meaning, as Magritte's canvas marks the presence and absence of

4 / Critical Paranoia: *El azar objetivo*

exterior and interior space. The poem ends again with a "carcajada metafísica," the laughter of the objects and the works of art that resist interpretation.

"Eupalinos," more than any other poem in *El azar objetivo*, exemplifies the paranoiac-critical method, which, by meticulously arranging apparently unrelated elements, reveals the contingency of rational constructs. The poem begins with a critique of the usual interpretation of the artist, the critic, or the philosopher: "Luego—decís—la contemplación de ese menguado tesoro / le niega la vida real—" (192) ["Therefore," you say, "the contemplation of that meager treasure / denies it real life"]. The speaker takes issue with this interpretation; the abstract thinker—be he artist, philosopher, mathematician, or scientist—rather, voluntarily distances himself from the complexity of life in order to create something "better" (in his mind), a pure and orderly vision of life.

> Mas bien él la convierte,
> de propia elección, en un estercolero,
> propiciado por tal epistemología de la basura;
> en efecto, la contempla como desde una altura excesiva,
> con supresión de todo oído y tacto,
> veía Fabrizio pasar los bueyes de reata,
> abejas de oro sobre las páginas de un salterio,
> con ese color miel pulido por la distancia;
> la contempla para irle robando como un entomólogo de opereta
> imágenes ligeras y fantasmas aéreos,
> fragmentos de porcelana, alfileres, medallas, los cuales
> son, mucho después, en la soledad de su mente
> una vida de mayor alcance.
>
> (192)

> [Rather, he converts it,
> of his choice, into a dungheap,
> propitiated by such an epistemology of rubbish;
> in effect, he contemplates it as, from an excessive height,
> suppressing all sound and touch,
> Fabrizio watched the oxen pass single file,
> golden bees upon the pages of a psaltery,
> with that honey color polished by the distance;
> he contemplates it to go about stealing from it, like an entomologist
>   from an operetta,
> light images and airy phantoms,

> fragments of porcelain, pins, medals, which
> are, much later, in the solitude of his mind,
> a life of greater scope.]

As in "La busca de la certeza," we see in this poem that the order imposed on reality from a contemplative distance only amounts to a pile of dung. The subject of the poem distances himself from the reality he observes, which allows him to purify the images he sees and to select only a few, pinning them down and giving them a coherent order in his mind. They become "una vida de mayor alcance" because they form—in his mind—a unified system that can be grasped, in contrast to the infinite multiplicity of "la vida real."

The metonymic connection between the images and allusions in this stanza, however, unbalances the unstable equilibrium of that system. First of all, the pure images of beauty that we encounter in the final lines are metonymically linked to the malodorous dungheap, rubbish, and oxen because they appear in the same stanza. The subject, like Fabrizio, may be distanced from this raw material, but the "pure" images are not (nor is the reader of this poem, especially if she has read the other poems in *El azar objetivo*). The word "como" is also problematic here, as it was in *Variaciones y figuras*, since it suggests the inaccuracy of images and allusions. Hence, the subject is not Fabrizio but *like* Fabrizio. And Fabrizio himself is problematic. Is he the entomologist Johann Christian Fabricius, as Jonathan Mayhew suggests, following the reference to entomology in the text,[8] or an operatic recreation of him? Or is he Fabrizio Carini Motta, the seventeenth-century Italian expert on theater architecture and stagecraft?[9] The references to the "opereta" and, later, to the architecture of Eupalinos would support the latter. We cannot resolve this enigma; thus the allusion to Fabrizio resists the kind of ordering system constructed by the subject, who is like Fabrizio. And, even if we could choose one Fabrizio or the other, we would still see only one aspect of his existence—his work and what it represents to us now—and not the infinite facets of his identity or his work (or the historical, philosophical, and biological contexts of his work, their relationship to our concepts of history, philosophy, and biology, etc.).[10] We still could not answer the question, "Who was Fabrizio?" Finally, the randomness of the images collected in the second half of the stanza suggests the instability of the order constructed from them; they have no necessary connection to one another, although we may impose one.

This chance connection is also highlighted in the remaining allusions and images of the poem. Why is Hatshepsuth included, and what is the significance of the handful of fertile seeds found with her funerary furnishings? We could think of any number of interpretations, I believe, in our attempts to impose an interpretative order upon this poem. The seeds themselves are fertile; does this suggest the fertility of the Egyptian culture, the sterility of culture in comparison to nature, the foresight and power of Egyptian religion and funerary rituals, or the limitations of all human constructions in the face of chance and time? The fertile seeds remain a mystery, despite the attempts of our fertile imaginations to create a symbolic meaning for them. The allusion to Hatshepsuth, like the seeds, appears random, irrational; we can make it fit one interpretation or another of the poem "Eupalinos," but only if we eliminate the other possibilities, following the methodology of our Fabrizio-like subject.

The poem begins and ends with Eupalinos, himself the literary creation of another author (Valéry), a figure who epitomizes the desire to improve and preserve reality by converting it into pure form. The lines that describe Eupalinos in this poem likewise progress from more detail to less, culminating in the "nitidez," or clarity, desired by the fictional architect:

>   Eupalinos
> alzó su templete redondo sobre cuatro columnas,
> imagen matemática de una muchacha de Corinto:
> no cuestiona él la legitimidad del procedimiento
> puesto que no se le alcanza ninguna alternativa posible
> pero obtiene con ello mayor nitidez
> en las imágenes (y una mayor gratificación afectiva,
> pues les da mayor nitidez)—
>   existencia
> equivale a gratificación afectiva
> acompañada de mayor nitidez—
>   ordena el caos
> de la vida real, tan inferior a su memoria,
> le confiere sentido y mayor nitidez.
>   (193)

>   [Eupalinos
> raised his round shrine upon four columns,
> the mathematical image of a girl from Corinth:
> he does not question the legitimacy of the procedure
> since he cannot grasp any possible alternative
> but he obtains with it greater clarity

in the images (and a greater affective gratification,
since it gives them greater clarity)—
                                        existence
equals affective gratification
accompanied by greater clarity—
                                  he orders the chaos
of real life, so inferior to his memory,
he endows it with meaning and greater clarity.]

Eupalinos creates, from a distance, a symbol of existence based upon certain premises of his culture: the premise that the girl from Corinth is beautiful; that the artist can and should represent beauty in clear images; that mathematics produces the clearest image; and that clarity produces the greatest emotional impact. He does not question any of these premises, from which his conclusion necessarily derives: "existencia / equivale a gratificación afectiva / acompañada de mayor nitidez." Likewise, he believes that the artist should represent life; therefore clarity and emotional impact are the key artistic goals. The reasoning is obviously circular, like the fishbowl of "Meditación de la pecera," and like that image, it does not account for the irrational or the unbeautiful—the seeds of Hatshepsuth, the multiple identity of Fabrizio, or the pile of dung.

In "De la inutilidad de los cristales ópticos" (194) [On the uselessness of eye glasses], that irrational element, like the stone from David's slingshot, destroys the Goliath of rational systems. The title, as my translation suggests, implies a play on the eyeglasses through which our subject observes the glass eyes of the stuffed animals in the "Museo de Historia Natural." The central image of the poem is the revolt of the animals, or the symbols, which the subject has immobilized through his analytical lens. At the end of this poem, their apparently inert glass eyes, explicitly linked to chance, shatter the eyeglasses of the person who attempts to impose order on and with them.

    Si las imágenes se apiñan en un recinto oscuro
    nada en ellas hay de movimiento (menos aún de hábito de movimiento);
    sí en cambio los ojos de cristal que el taxidermista tan bien conoce,
    con su excesiva holgura en la órbita seca;
    un día han de invadir a medianoche
    los bulevares de la ciudad desierta,
    aterrando con su agilidad a los animales pacíficos,
    en una conjunción única que consagre el azar.

4 / Critical Paranoia: *El azar objetivo* 113

> El azar, aniquilando en su represalia de hondero
> el estupor del que alinea y su conciso cristal.
>
> (194)

> [If the images crowd together in an obscure space
> there is nothing of movement in them (and even less of habit of movement);
> there is, however, in the glass eyes that the taxidermist knows so well,
> with their excessive ease in the dry socket;
> one day they are destined to invade at midnight
> the boulevards of the deserted city,
> terrorizing the peaceful animals with their agility,
> in a unique conjunction consecrated by chance.
>
> Chance, annihilating in its slingshot retaliation
> the stupor of the one who aligns and his concise glass.]

The brevity of this poem represents how suddenly and violently the safe, orderly theories and systems of analysis delineated in the preceding four poems may be shattered by chance.

"El azar objetivo" summarizes the argument of the book and thus serves as its conclusion. The subject continues to construct empty rational structures from selected details: these systems seem, from a distance, to resolve the enigmas of life, but in fact they only ignore them. Several words in the opening stanzas emphasize the sterility of this method: "vacío" [empty], "no ve" [does not see], "vacua" [vacuous]. The subject does not question his method, however, only the efficacy with which he implements it:

> Y con todo
> palpa ausencias que achaca no a la nulidad del procedimiento
> sino a limitación de la memoria,
> olvido de algún fragmento significativo que ponga
> en solución aquella maquinaria,
> o bien a su impericia combinatoria, que hubiera
> de suplirlo, ante un número suficiente aunque corto
> de datos dispersos.
>
> (195)

> [And with all that
> he feels absences that he blames not on the nullity of the method
> but on the limitations of memory,
> the forgetting of some significant fragment that could set

that mechanism right,
or on his combinatorial ineptitude, that must be
overlooked, given a sufficient though scant number
of dispersed data.]

The end of the poem, like the conclusion of a critical essay, repeats the thesis: rational systems may easily be destroyed by the irrational elements that they cannot or choose not to perceive:

> Depende,
> aunque lo ignora, de una sola pisada que, sonando,
> los desordene, y concluya de ese modo en azar su imagen cierta;
> resonando en el empedrado de un pasadizo estrecho
> dicte un ritmo a la memoria, y su cochambre
> se anule, suscitando los reales fantasmas,
> derogación del fetichismo tácito que llamamos "presente"
> cuyo prestigio vulneran los enigmas
> que, invadiendo la memoria, suscita el azar, y a veces resuelve.
>
> (196)

> [It depends,
> although he is unaware of it, upon a single footstep that, striking,
> may disorder them, and his certain image thus fall by chance;
> resonating on the stone pavement of a narrow passage
> it may dictate a rhythm to memory, and his filth
> be nullified, raising the real phantoms,
> derogation of the tacit fetishism we call "present"
> whose prestige is discredited by the enigmas
> that, invading the memory, chance awakens and sometimes resolves.]

This moment of destruction is the breakthrough of objective chance, which disorders rational systems but clarifies enigmas through an irrational epiphany.

This conclusion brings us full circle, back to "El juego lúgubre" and the epiphany afforded by Dalí's paranoiac-critical method in the realm of objective chance, so we may well wonder to what extent Carnero has poetically replicated Dalí's method in *El azar objetivo*. Certainly, the book uses a formal logic (structure, objective discourse) in conjunction with an ontological illogic (the irrational elements that occur randomly) to parody and criticize traditional, comfortable systems of thought. Yet despite the marauding animals, the eye-slinging and the excrement, this book lacks the ferocity and complete irreverence of surrealism. This is due, in part, to the postmodern writer's recognition of the limitations of the avant-garde, which has either self-destructed or become mainstream.[11] Thus, the repetition in this book of the number three—reminiscent of the triple, three-part, three-stage surrealist revolution—may remind us that even revolutionary movements constitute ordering systems and that the tenets of even the avant-garde revolution were derived from the very system it sought to destroy. In "El juego lúgubre" Carnero asserted that Dalí transcended those limitations by systematizing paranoia; in his poetry, however, Carnero places in doubt the concept of the independent individual psyche that could generate an artistic vision unconnected to its cultural context or unfettered by the contingency of the artistic medium. An intertextual reading of *El azar objetivo* and "El juego lúgubre" suggests that poetry and criticism, by drawing attention to their own premises and lacunae, can foreground the dialectic between rationality and irrationality, order and chaos, "que por falta de centro no termina" (189) [which for lack of a center never ends].

5

In Retrospect:
Divisibilidad indefinida

GUILLERMO Carnero's most recent book, *Divisibilidad indefinida* [Indefinite divisibility], appeared in 1990, eleven years after the publication of *Ensayo de una teoría de la visión,* and fifteen years after he published the last book of that anthology, *El azar objetivo.* In the course of those years, Spain underwent a tremendous metamorphosis: Francisco Franco died; the dictatorship ended; a constitutional democracy was established and a socialist prime minister came to rule; censorship abated; cultural frontiers opened; and many exiles returned.

Spanish poetry also changed dramatically during the period following Franco's death.[1] Critics largely agree upon the characteristics of the *posnovísimo* poetry that emerged at this time, perhaps because they feel less obliged to "define" it and are content to simply describe its heterogeneous forms.[2] Opposed to the *culturalismo* of their immediate predecessors, these poets prefer to write a personal poetry of experience, to "sacudirse el *polvo bárbaramente intelectual* de la biblioteca" [to shake off the *barbarously intellectual dust* of the library] and return to the world, "la vida normal."[3] Another trait of *posnovísimo* poetry is the return to classical forms, meter and rhyme, a departure from the free forms and unrhymed verses of the previous generation. Two other tendencies of this generation have their roots in *novísimo* poetics. One of these is the creation by some poets of "mundos clausurados y emblemáticos" [closed up and emblematic worlds][4] through the use of repetition and metonymy, a type of poetry that seems a natural development of the techniques elaborated in *Dibujo de la muerte.* The other is the poetics of silence, which takes two forms: (1) the critique of poetic language, exemplified by Carnero's *Variaciones* and *Azar;* and (2) minimalism, "esa tendencia de supresión, síntesis, brevedad, concisión, elusión, sugerencia, espacios blancos en la disposición tipográfica de la página, etc." [that tendency toward suppression, synthesis, brevity, conciseness, elusion, suggestiveness, blank spaces in the layout of the page, etc.].[5]

The *novísimo* poets who continued to write during the 1980s incorporated into their poetry many of the techniques favored by the younger generation. For example, several poets participated in the two forms of the poetics of silence:

> concisión extremada, manipulación de textos y materiales, injertos aforísticos o narrativos (José Miguel Ullán, Félix de Azúa, Aníbal Núñez) y, en general, concentración, síntesis, minimalismo (el Gimferrer de *Com un epíleg*, José Luis Jover, Jaime Siles, Andrés Trapiello).[6]

> [extreme conciseness, manipulation of texts and materials, aphoristic or narrative graftings (José Miguel Ullán, Félix de Azúa, Aníbal Núñez) and, in general, concentration, synthesis, minimalism (the Gimferrer of *Com un epíleg*, José Luis Jover, Jaime Siles, Andrés Trapiello).]

Nicolás notes that Gimferrer and Siles employed yet another form of this poetry, one that, departing from the mystical and romantic traditions, treats silence as a theme.[7] The remaining *novísimo* poets contributed to the poetics of silence in a more dramatic way by seriously degenerating or by ceasing to publish poetry, as in the cases of Leopoldo María Panero and Guillermo Carnero.[8]

Carnero emerged from his silence in 1990 with the publication of *Divisibilidad indefinida*. This book is highly lyrical, and it features a speaker who is closely identified with Carnero himself; he is a poet reviewing his poetic career. It also employs a traditional form, the sonnet, for the first time in Carnero's published poetry. *Divisibilidad* resembles *posnovísimo* poetry, then, in the use of a more personal lyrical voice and of a traditional form.

Despite this tenuous connection to *posnovísimo* poetry, *Divisibilidad indefinida* does not embrace the aesthetics of the younger generation. As always in Carnero's poems, the references to the lyricism and forms of pure poetry are more ironic and critical than adulatory, reflecting the poet's skepticism regarding rational, linguistic, and poetic orders. In fact, Carnero's linguistic and philosophical interests make a "naive" personal poetics impossible for him: he simply does not believe that any linguistic structure can so easily embody a meaning, an experience, or an emotion, since "produce el lenguaje sus propios fantasmas / que proyectados hacia atrás inventan una realidad posible / de que ellos serían reflejo" [language produces its own phantasms / which projected backwards invent a possible reality / of which they would be the reflection].[9] For Carnero, any "personal" issues in poetry must be filtered through the lens of philosophy and linguistic theory, and framed by poetic structures.

Divisibilidad indefinida is a retrospective book: it refers back to all of Carnero's previous poetry, as well as to poetic conventions from the medieval period through modernism, including the convention of retrospective literature itself.[10] Connections to Carnero's earlier work abound in this text. The metonymic images of *Dibujo de la muerte* are once again prominent, linked to the problem of the sign, social order, and personal identity. Many of the images that have appeared throughout Carnero's poetry (night, light and its reflection and refraction in mirrors and water, birds, and gardens) also recur here, along with the lyricism and neoclassical allusions of *Dibujo de la muerte*, a self-critical, ironic speaker reminiscent of *El sueño de Escipión*, and certain key figures from *El azar objetivo* (particularly the glass eyes of mummified animals) that recall the potential threat of those deceptively docile forms that we manipulate to construct rational meanings. And, as in *Azar*, the mutability of forms is suggested here even on the level of the phoneme, primarily through an alliterative practice that signals absence as well as presence. Even the fixed pattern of *Divisibilidad*—the fivefold repetition of two sonnets followed by a longer poem constituted mostly of unrhymed quatrains—has a precedent in the lexical, semantic, and formal repetitions of *Variaciones y figuras sobre un tema de La Bruyère*. These connections to Carnero's previous work bring to mind the philosophical issues explored there, such as the contingency of identity, the death of the author, and the fragility of stultified linguistic, personal, poetic, and rational forms.

Divisibilidad indefinida also alludes, sometimes obliquely, to the conventions of the lyric, and it undermines those conventions by commenting ironically upon them and by placing them in the context of a historical development of aesthetic and philosophical theory; their apparently permanent orders are thus seen as steps in the development of an increasing alienation in the human arts and psyche. For example, the ironic citation in "Fantasía de un amanecer de invierno" (21–24)[11] [Fantasy of a winter's dawn] of a line from the thirteenth century *Libro de Alexandre*—"A sílabas contadas, que es [de] gran maestría" [in counted syllables, which is a great skill]—undercuts the culturalist pretensions of that work and of the structured verse itself.[12] That verse comes to represent the state of humanity—measured, orderly, and utterly cut off from the presence of the world. In addition to this allusion to medieval poetics, *Divisibilidad* evokes Renaissance lyric by the use of the sonnet form, a lyrical voice, and an initial epigraph from Fernando de Herrera's *Anotaciones a Garcilaso*. In the Renaissance, the sonnet form represented an eternal, unified order in which the lyric speaker participated. In the sonnets of Carnero's book, however, irrational images, structural breaks, and explicit critiques of form undermine that illusion of plenitude, integrity, and stability. The rigid order of the sonnets is also destabilized by the relationship between those poems and the long, unstructured ones, which recur periodically throughout the book and tend to fragment the images of the sonnets and comment ironically upon them and their illusory order. The longer poems also unravel the meaning and form of the sonnets because, like the "variaciones" of *Variaciones y figuras*, they reincorporate time into the interpretive process, melting the frozen images and forms of the sonnets.[13] The form of the long poems also recalls aesthetic changes in the lyric dating from the romantic period; in this way, they suggest a historical retrospection as well (the romantic commenting upon the Neoplatonic).

In fact, this book contains implicit and explicit references to medieval, renaissance, neoclassical, romantic, and modernist poetry; these allusions suggest the historicity of poetics (as in the measured verse and the sonnet form) and of concepts of the self.[14] It is here that a personal, lyrical emotion comes into play, that is, in the relationship between philosophy, poetics, and the self. In *Divisibilidad indefinida*, the speaker is identified with these issues by his conversion into a linguistic sign—a word, a structure, a text, a group of texts—that initially represents plenitude but becomes fragmented through the philosophical developments of the modern age, and is perhaps finally restored. In "Lección del páramo" (9) [Lesson of the wasteland], the speaker is equated with the images he observes through their act of writing— "escriben"—and his coexistence with them on the same ontological plane. At the beginning of "Música para fuegos de artificio" (13–15) [Fireworks music], words have the same sense of presence as the speaker; thus, when they are fragmented and dispersed, he is as well. He and his words are mechanized and frozen in "Fantasía de un amanecer de invierno," "Los motivos del jardín" (29–32) [The motives of the garden], and "Divisibilidad indefinida" (37–40). His beloved is a fractured sign in "Convento de Santo Tomé" (19) [Convent of Saint Tomé], and the speaker literally becomes a book in "Catedral de Avila" (35) [Cathedral in Avila]. This speaker, this linguistic sign, this construction of intertexual connections and philosophical conflicts, despairs of his loss of meaning and coherence, dies, and is, perhaps, revived in the final poem of the book. This is a far cry from confessional poetry, but the emotional impact is profound and devastating.

The first poem of *Divisibilidad indefinida*, "Lección del páramo," is an example of the ways in which the book establishes a connection between the speaker and the historical fragmentation of poetic conventions, Carnero's previous work, and the topos of literary retrospection. In this poem, the conventions that have traditionally represented permanence and presence—images, alliteration, a prominent lyrical speaker, the sonnet form, consonant rhyme (ABBA AbBA CDE CDE, the pattern of seven of the ten sonnets in this book)—come to signal change and absence.

>   Veo cruzar el pájaro pausado
>   por el aire que apenas dividido
>   se suelda sin estela de sonido
>   en su cristal ardiente y deslumbrado
>
>   y un arroyo que mudo e ignorado
>   en el valle perdido
>   minimiza el caudal de su latido
>   y lo conduce al arenal quemado.
>
>   Ave y arroyo son mi compañía
>   y su vuelo y fluir faltos de historia,
>   nunca pensado ni jamás oído,
>
>   escriben que es bastante melodía
>   el cofre sin abrir de la memoria
>   y el laberinto ciego del sentido.

(9)

>   [I see the bird deliberately cross
>   through the air that scarcely divided
>   sews itself up without a wake of a sound
>   in its burning and blinded crystal
>
>   and a brook that mute and unknown
>   in the lost valley
>   minimizes the flow of its beating
>   and guides it to the burning sands.

5 / In Retrospect: *Divisibilidad indefinida*

> Bird and brook are my companions
> and their flight and flow free of history
> never thought nor ever heard,
>
> they write that melody enough is
> the unopened coffer of memory
> and the blind labyrinth of sense.]

The relationship between the speaker and the other images of the poem is established in the first two stanzas: he is the only witness to their ephemeral existence. He is more fully identified with them in the tercets, in which they are his companions and fellow authors—"escriben." They are also linked by their coexistence as linguistic signs in the poem "Lección del páramo."

In order to understand the speaker's identity, then, we must examine those other signs, which are identified with him. In the first stanza, the bird's flight produces a barely divisible crack in the sky that appears and disappears without a trace; thus the alliteration there points not to presence but to the tension between absence and presence in the image.[15] It also draws attention to the linguistic nature of the image and thus suggests the absence of the referent in the sign, since "language is, as it were, that which *divides* reality."[16] And the signs themselves point to absence. Even the traces of the symbolic bird, like those of language and of interpretation, soon disappear: after its brief flight, "el aire . . . apenas dividido / se suelda sin estela de sonido." The brook also evaporates quickly: "mudo e ignorado" it wanders through the "valle perdido" and disappears in the "arenal quemado."

These images have had similar implications throughout Carnero's literary work. The bird image, for example, recalls the ultimately uninterpretable "palomas" in "Muerte en Venecia," which merged with the night, the water, Spinell's hands, the wind, and the piano. A bird also figured prominently in "Sotheby's," the third variation of *Variaciones y figuras*, where it symbolized the limits of interpretation. The brook likewise recalls Carnero's earlier poetry: water was a hidden fountain, representing the limits of knowledge, and a surface that only reflected our inquiring faces and hopelessly refracted reality ("Muerte en Venecia," "Les charmes de la vie," "Investigación de una doble metonimia"). Significantly, this image appeared with that of the bird in "Sotheby's," and, again, it suggested the limits of interpretation, of the sign, represented by the stationary bird that cast its shadow upon the water but captured only a small portion of it. The greatest part of reality escaped interpretation, and the fragment momentarily frozen by it suggested the absence of the rest. This intertextuality with Carnero's previous poetry revives the issue of the limited sign by allusion and by example, since even the apparently stable images of "Lección del páramo" are not limited to this text but suggest a multiplicity of possible meanings and referents beyond it.

The reference to acts of writing ("escriben"), in conjunction with the sonnet form and the discussion of the limits of the sign, foregrounds the development of concepts of order, literary structure, and personal integrity from the Renaissance to the present.[17] The sonnet form itself and the reference to Garcilaso in the epigraph of the book bring to mind a Neoplatonic concept of an orderly, harmonious external reality into which human beings should seek to integrate themselves: the sonnet reflects that order and the lyric speaker participates in it. The tercets, however, highlight the absence of time and history in that concept, and the references to *memoria* and sense point to a Heideggerian critique of such ordering systems, especially the Cartesian imposition of orders, derived from a subjective rationality, upon the unruly passions of the self and upon an essentially chaotic world. The sonnet, then, would represent that type of order, existing or derived from within and imposed upon the external world, and it is exactly the kind of frozen form that will be criticized in other poems of this volume.

"Lección del páramo," while connecting with these contradictory traditions, proposes another possibility: the self reflects the chaos of the world, the absence of fixed meaning, the temporality of experience. Thus the broken sonnet form reflects the irrationality of the self and the world, represented here in the structural break that mirrors the winding brook that cannot be contained by form. This identification between the speaker and the irrational undermines Neoplatonic and neoclassical concepts of the lyrical speaker, since here he is neither the reflection nor the creator of a harmonious and orderly natural scene, and it anticipates the resolution offered in the final poem of the book, "La hacedora de lluvia" [The rainmaker].

This is the lesson learned from the wasteland, which may also be the lesson learned from *The Waste Land* (1922), T. S. Eliot's long, retrospective poem. The alienation in that poem, like that of *Divisibilidad indefinida*, is the product of the limitations of modern Western thought, which is represented by allusion and by contrast to Eastern paradigms. The title of Carnero's poem, "*Lección* del páramo," suggests a historical relationship between Eliot and Carnero. The postmodernism of Carnero is *learned*, in a sense, from the postromantic, postneoclassical, post-Renaissance poetics, as well as from the alienation, of Eliot. The allusion to *The Waste Land* may also be seen to refer tangentially to the form, preoccupations, and multiple allusions of that long, unstructured poem. All of this brings to mind, once again, the historical shifts in the definition of the meaning and locus of order and, subsequently, in the relationship between the self and nature, emotion and reason, leading to the chaos of the postmodern moment, and the fragility of this speaker, who, in contrast to Eliot, offers no alternative cultural paradigm, no seamless other.

The relationship between presence and absence, order and chaos, unity and fragmentation, in the world and in the self, is represented in the images, phonemes, and structure of "Música para fuegos de artificio." In this poem the speaker's identity and the development of Western aesthetic ideas are tied to the images and the linguistic sign, which initially represent presence but come to signify fragmentation and absence. A historical development is suggested by the allusions to Handel's *Royal Fireworks Music* (1750) and to Rubén Darío's "Yo soy aquel" (1905) [I am he], as well as by the looser poetic structure (unrhymed verses of eleven and fourteen syllables in one quintet, nine quatrains, and a tercet) more reminiscent of romanticism than neoclassicism. The relative lack of pattern here is also significant because it provides a contrast to the rigid order of the preceding sonnets and thus signals the dissolution of those structured systems of meaning.

"Música para fuegos de artificio" begins with the allusion to Darío's famous poem and to a past sense of presence:

>Hace muy pocos años yo decía
>palabras refulgentes como piedras preciosas
>y veía rodar, como un milagro
>abombado y azul, la gota tenue
>por el cabello rubio hacia la espalda.
>
>No eran palabras frágiles, prendidas al azar
>de un evadido vuelo prescindible,
>sino plenas y grávidas victorias
>en las que ver el mundo y obtenerlo.
>
>La emoción de enunciar un orden justo
>cedía realidad al sonido y al tacto
>y quedaba en los labios la certeza
>de conocer en el sabor y el nombre.

(13)

> [Only a few years ago I pronounced
> words radiant as precious stones
> and I saw roll, like a miracle,
> convex and blue, the tenuous drop
> through the blond hair toward the back.
>
> They were not fragile words, grasped by chance
> from an extraneous evaded flight,
> but full and weighty victories
> in which to see the world and obtain it.
>
> The emotion of enunciating a just order
> ceded reality to sound and touch
> and there remained on my lips the certainty
> of knowing in the taste and the name.]

These stanzas speak of a moment of linguistic, poetic and personal plenitude, which appears not only in the solid images ("plenas y grávidas victorias," "un orden justo," "el sabor y el nombre"), but also in the alliteration of these first stanzas: the repetition of the consonants *p, v, c,* and *s* gives the lines more presence and suggests a relationship among the words in which they appear, thereby creating a linguistic order. The speaker participates physically in the richness of this linguistic presence, which touches all his senses.

This plenitude dissipates in the following stanzas, leaving only traces of presence, which flash briefly and disappear.

> Pero la certidumbre de una mirada limpia
> es una ingenuidad no perdurable,
> y el viento arrastra en ráfagas de crespones y agujas
> el vicio de creer envuelto en polvo.
>
> Y si tras de la luz esplendorosa
> que pone en pie la vida en un haz de palmeras
> el miedo de dormir cierra los cálices
> susurrando promesas de una luz sucesiva,
>
> el fulgor de la fe lento se orienta
> al imán de la noche permanente
> en la que tacto, imagen y sonido
> flotan en la quietud de lo sinónimo,

5 / In Retrospect: *Divisibilidad indefinida*

> sin temor de mortales travesías
> ni los dones que otorga la torpeza
> sino un fugaz vislumbre de medusas:
> inconsistentes ecos reiterados
>
> en un reino de paz y pericia,
> apagado jardín de la memoria
> donde inertes se pudren sumergidos
> los oropeles del conocimiento. . . .
>
> (14)

> [But the certainty of a clear gaze
> is a naïveté that cannot last,
> and the wind drags off in gusts of crepe and needles
> the vice of believing wrapped in dust.
>
> And if after the resplendent light
> that life puts forth in a ray of palm trees
> the fear of sleeping closes off the chalices
> whispering promises of successive light
>
> the flash of faith slowly orients itself
> to the magnet of the permanent night
> in which touch, image and sound
> float in the quietude of the synonymous,
>
> without fear of mortal crossings
> nor the gifts bestowed by torpidity
> but a fleeting glimpse of medusas:
> inconsistent echoes reiterated
>
> in a realm of peace and proficiency,
> extinguished garden of memory
> where, inert and submerged, rots
> the tinsel of knowledge. . . .]

The speaker's observations and the images imply that a philosophical cataclysm has shattered the earlier linguistic plenitude into "inconsistentes ecos reiterados." Those echoes are represented in the continuing alliteration—as when fear hisses like the biblical serpent, "susurrando promesas de una luz sucesiva," and even the dissipation of his vision ironically continues to repeat the *p* of its promise in the words "apagado," "pudren," and "oropeles."

The same letters that earlier represented a shining presence here represent the discarded tinsel, or fireworks, which provide only transient and fragmentary relief from the fearful night and foreground further the depth of that void. The speaker cannot reconstruct the original image of light from these multitudinous slivers dispersed in the sky; thus, the comfort and fullness of his original vision of light give way at the end of the poem to a frightful darkness and disintegration: "quien hace oficio de nombrar el mundo / forja al fin un fervor erosionado / en la noche total definitiva" (15) [he who makes it his business to name the world / forges at last an eroded fervor / in the total, definitive night].

The destruction of the speaker's original vision of language and reality has a profound effect upon his personal integrity, since a coherent identity is based upon a stable relationship between oneself and the world. Thus at the beginning of the poem, the speaker could believe in the unity and coherence of his own existence, as reflected in the word: "quedaba en los labios la certeza / de conocer en el sabor y el nombre." When he recognizes the distance between poetic images and the reality they seek to represent, when that symbolic order crumbles, the speaker also becomes dissociated from plenitude and hopelessly fragmented into "inconsistentes ecos reiterados."

This movement from plenitude to loss represents the philosophical shift from unity between self and world to alienation. The image of the "palmeras," in conjunction with the discussion of the word and light, recalls the belief, dating from the Book of Genesis, in the absolute identity between enunciation and creation, between the word and the object. In Handel's day, there was a similar faith in *man*'s ability to impose a structure upon reality, to create the world in that sense.[18] Still, in the neoclassical period, the human mind is dissociated from the world, which becomes an unruly other that must be ordered and controlled. There also occurs a radical split between reason and the passions, which, like nature, are controlled by the structures of the mind. The allusion in the opening lines to Rubén Darío's retrospective poem, "Yo soy aquel," suggests a critique of this modern split as well as an example of the resultant divided self, since Darío autobiographically comments in that poem upon his own earlier poetic practice—its lyricism, Parnassianism, and purity. In other words, the mature Darío is divided against his own youthful self. "Música" reflects these divisions, and it is in this sense that the self, the speaker of this poem, becomes both internally fragmented and alienated from the world.

This split is represented in many of the sonnets as a disjuncture between "figure" (the interpretive ordering form imposed upon matter) and "presence" or being. In "Convento de Santo Tomé" (19) such a division appears to take place only within the chiseled artistic figure described there, the "tú," and between that "tú" and the speaker. However, this apparently external division represents an interior fragmentation as well, leading to the living death of the speaker.

From the beginning of the poem, the "tú" is linked to a static vision of art and of the linguistic sign, that is, of forms imposed upon material by the rational mind:

> Después de tantos años tu figura
> no ha perdido una tilde de belleza
> ni el sereno posar de tu cabeza
> o la fragilidad de tu armadura,
>
> ni tu rostro desmiente su tersura
> ni tu serena frente su nobleza
> ni tus ojos la paz y la entereza
> forjada en fe sin lastre de cordura.
>
> [After so many years, your figure
> has not lost a tilde of beauty
> nor the serene repose of your head
> or the fragility of your armor,
>
> nor does your face deny its smoothness
> nor your serene forehead its nobility
> nor your eyes the peace and integrity
> forged in faith without weight of judgment.]

It is an image of peace and order, but not of life, because the figure is static and limited, dissociated from presence; thus in the tercets we read: "tú moriste de un golpe de tu muerte" [you died at one blow from your death].[19]

The separation of presence and figure within the work of art has profound implications for the speaker's integrity for several reasons. The speaker sees that work as an "other," a "tú": this division in itself reflects the philosophical problem that eventually leads to modern and postmodern alienation, that is, the dissociation between self and other, mind and matter, reason and emotion, figure and presence. This split makes the speaker's fragmentation inevitable, especially if we consider that this "tú" is specifically the *speaker's* other: she also has a human form, and he sees himself in her image: "por igualdad contraria de destino / tú moriste de un golpe de tu muerte, / yo he muerto lentamente de mi vida" [by an inverse equality of destiny / you died at one blow from your death, / I have died slowly from my life]. The parallel construction of the final two verses and the words "por igualdad" reinforce the connection between the speaker and the "tú." What is more, both are ephemeral linguistic creations: the speaker only exists within this poem, and the images of the beloved's features are likewise purely textual and ephemeral, prefaced by "ni." The reference to the tilde in the first stanza even suggests that she is literally the word "tú," the linguistic sign of the other. "Convento de Santo Tomé," then, shows that, by dividing the self and the world, rationalism has effaced presence and replaced it with empty figures, ordering systems that refract plenitude and reflect a lack of meaning. It has also produced an inner split, dividing the self against itself and the world.

"Lección del agua" also explains that the fragmentation of reality implies a concomitant incoherence in the image of the speaker and his textual (self-)representation, despite (and in part because of) the rigid sonnet form.

> Mirándome en el agua de la fuente
> por salvar las imágenes vencidas
> —colores idos, músicas caídas—
> en memoria con gracia de presente
>
> las vi oscilar girando levemente
> en facetas y trizas esparcidas
> recompuestas y luego divididas,
> y hundirse y escapar en la corriente.
>
> Puse sobre las aguas un espejo
> con que hurtarme a la muerte en escritura
> y retener la luz de la conciencia
>
> pero la nada duplicó el reflejo
> y el cristal añadió su veladura
> en doble fraude de la trasparencia.

(33)

> [Looking at myself in the water of the fountain
> to save the vanquished images
> —faded colors, fallen music—
> in memory with the grace of presence

5 / In Retrospect: *Divisibilidad indefinida*   129

> I saw them oscillate revolving lightly
> in facets and scattered fragments
> recomposed and later divided,
> and sink and escape in the current.
>
> I put a mirror upon the waters
> with which to steal myself from death in writing
> and retain the light of consciousness
>
> but nothingness duplicated the reflection
> and the crystal added its glaze
> in a double fraud of transparency.]

The structure of the Renaissance sonnet generally implies order and harmony, as the problem proposed in the quatrains is resolved in the tercets. In this poem, the quatrains describe the refraction of the speaker on the surface of the water, the world, in which he hoped to see his reflection. In the tercets he attempts to restore his image through writing, but the representation of writing as a mirror creates an image of infinite regression, of one mirror surface reflecting another. Thus, the tercets do not resolve the problem of the quatrains; they only reflect and refract it, serving as the "igualdad contraria" of the earlier "Convento de Santo Tomé." This sonnet creates an illusory order, a surface that is a reflection of infinite fragmentation, of nothing, of the speaker.[20]

"Fantasía de un amanecer de invierno" and "Los motivos del jardín" demonstrate how the imposition of rationality on the world has reduced it to a mechanical object, devoid of mystery—again, a figure without presence. Both poems focus on attempts to create a rational order, which we then claim to have discovered in nature.[21] In "Fantasía" the use of irony mocks the rational and poetic ordering of reality, which gives us only an illusory comfort. In that poem, the coherence of the speaker becomes further identified with those linguistic orders: he literally becomes the word, part of a text that may be scanned and counted. In "Los motivos del jardín" he is the creator of his own circular ordering system, like the neoclassical garden of the title and the one described in Carnero's "Jardín inglés" *(El sueño de Escipión),* in which he attempts to reflect the perfect shape of the sun. The human inventions in the garden, however—a weathervane, language, a rectangular window—refract the spherical light, and the garden itself is a limited and limiting rational structure. A perfect reflection of natural order is also undermined by the mechanical quality, restrictiveness, and artificiality of human ordering systems, suggested by the words "Finge," "autómata," "confinados," "ejercicio de transfiguración," "máquina de fingir," "miente" [Feigns, automaton, confined, exercise of transfiguration, pretend machine, lies]. As a result of the mechanization of the world and its fragmentation in the garden, the speaker is alienated, cognizant of the grotesque deformation of presence implicit in the circular figures—"figurillas"—that include the garden, language, and poetic form, but he is unable to free himself from them.

In "Divisibilidad indefinida" those figures, devoid of presence, become further fragmented and frozen, and the speaker finds himself similarly paralyzed. The images are refracted by their metonymic connections to the three forms of water represented here—the brook, the drop, and ice. For example, light is frozen; arches hide the "invisible hielo" [invisible ice]; the eyes of the lynx and the tiger, though dead, reflect and refract reality; the petal is punished by water; the bird petrifies the stream; the place in which the speaker lives is colorless; the droplets echo; and "los metales preciosos / de la abyección y del conocimiento" [the precious metals / of abjection and knowledge] are frozen. The images of decay and ice, the effect of time's passing, are constant throughout the poem; thus, although the lengthy description of a seemingly natural scene may bring to mind the *locus amoenus* of Renaissance verse, the immobility and silence in this poem are paradoxically disquieting:

> Fluye el silencio en ondas de blancura
> desde sus doce aristas minerales
> donde se encierra congelada y turbia
> la inerte vacuidad cristalizada
>
> y así crece la paz, sorda y entera
> en haces de fulgor estrangulado
> hasta la ojiva de invisible hielo
> donde convergen mansos y se anudan.
>
> [Silence flows in waves of whiteness
> from its twelve mineral angles
> where, frozen and clouded,
> the inert, crystallized emptiness confines itself
>
> and thus grows peace, deaf and whole,
> in beams of strangled flashes

5 / In Retrospect: *Divisibilidad indefinida*

>   to the ogive of invisible ice
>   where they tamely converge and unite.]

The peace described here is bought at a high price—frozen knowledge, arrested thought, and the death by strangulation of the "haces de fulgor" from "Música para fuegos de artificio." Especially in the context of *El azar objetivo*, it is clear that this image represents a critique of rationality. As in "Convento de Santo Tomé," the anthropomorphic description of those fragments of presence suggests that they are reflections of this speaker and, more generally, of a moribund humanity, trapped by the words and forms that our rational constructs have piled up and frozen. The speaker hopes for a way to melt those frozen forms and restore the fractured light.

>   ¿Quién quebrará las puertas de la luz?
>
>   Un calor que licúe los metales preciosos
>   de la abyección y del conocimiento, un pie
>   grácil que humille y desordene
>   las palabras caídas que el miedo y la belleza
>   amontonan y pudren en su otoño,
>   una voz como cúpula dorada
>   combando el clarear del sol naciente,
>   la que descorre el velo,
>   la que trae de vuelta al alejado.
>
>   [Who will break down the doors of light?
>
>   A warmth that could melt the precious metals
>   of abjection and knowledge, a slender foot
>   that could humble and disorder
>   the fallen words that fear and beauty
>   pile up and rot in their autumn,
>   a voice like a golden dome
>   bending the dawning of the rising sun,
>   the one that draws the veil,
>   the one that brings back the distant.]

The language here is clearly reminiscent of modernism, especially of Juan Ramón Jiménez in the use of the infinitive and of Jorge Guillén in the image of perfection. The work of these two poets would seem to represent the kind of temporal and spatial immobility that this poem criticizes. The speaker hopes for an end to such alienation, but the use of the subjunctive indicates that he has not found, and perhaps will never find, the way out of this philosophical dead end. Where is that warmth, that foot, that voice? The slenderness suggests a female form, which was associated with art, the passions, and the speaker in "Convento de Santo Tomé" and with mystery and irrationality in "Meditación de la pecera" *(El azar objetivo)*. The beauty of the final image, described in the indicative, stands as a glimmer of hope, of presence, much like the alliteration, form, and imagery of the preceding poems.

This hope is apparently fulfilled in "La hacedora de lluvia," the last poem of the book, in which the speaker dies, loses his fictitious, orderly self, and is revived by a dark, fluid, feminine form, the healed and healing "other" of "Convento de Santo Tomé." At the beginning of the poem, the speaker's alienation has finally destroyed him:

> Al borde del camino yace el hombre quemado
> bajo una tenue túnica de polvo
> que el viento deshilacha y teje
> como la mano lenta que sosiega al dormido.
>
> Recubiertos de sal sus ojos miran
> la redonda quietud del horizonte,
> arista viva contra el seco párpado,
> hiriente como gota que no puede abreviarse,
>
> ni la oquedad del cielo en que resuena
> con una [*sic*] leve chirrido de juguete mecánico
> la descomposición de la memoria,
> marcada por la luz del negro al oro.

(45)

> [On the edge of the road lies the burned man
> beneath a tenuous tunic of dust
> that the wind unravels and weaves
> like the slow hand that lulls the sleeper.
>
> Covered over with salt his eyes look at
> the round quietude of the horizon,
> living edge against the dry eyelid,
> wounding like a drop that cannot be reduced

> nor the cavity of the sky in which resounds
> with the slight creaking of a mechanical toy
> the decomposition of memory,
> marked by the light from black to gold.]

The scene described is one of utter desolation. The speaker has become one with his world, but it is the ahistorical, mechanical world of his own creation, and the result has been his own paralyzation and death. Several images from preceding poems recur here as signs to wound the man: fireworks, circularity, a drop of water, and memory cause him physical pain. The image is as sensorial as that of "Música," but instead of victory we see here the most absolute defeat.

In the final stanzas of the poem, the speaker begins to be healed when he merges with a fluid female figure.

> Ondulante el cabello como curso de agua
> que perezoso se bifurca y pierde
> por el redondo cauce que muere en la cadera,
>
> sus ojos negros pesan como nubes oscuras
> aquietando el rumor de la tormenta
> retenido al antojo de la luz
> que se amansa a la sombra de sus párpados.
>
> Y se tiende desnuda como un río
> ovillado y redondo, cuyas aguas oscuras
> ungen los huesos yertos, la sima de la boca,
> y humedecen los ojos apagados.
>
> [With her hair flowing like the water's path
> that lazily forks and loses itself
> in the round riverbed that dies at the hip,
>
> her black eyes weigh down like dark clouds
> quieting the sound of the storm
> held back at the whim of the light
> that becomes tame at the shadow of her eyelids.
>
> And she stretches out naked like a river
> rolled up and round, whose dark waters

> anoint his motionless bones, the chasm of his mouth,
> and moisten his extinguished eyes.]

These stanzas point to a reintegration, a healing of the split between the speaker and the "tu," the speaker and the world, but this type of integrity is only possible after death, after the Cartesian worldview has been extinguished.

The poems of *Divisibilidad indefinida*, then, trace the consequences of modern Western philosophy through the figure of the speaker, who passes from plenitude through fragmentation to a possible reintegration into plenitude. The intertextuality with Carnero's work, along with the irony of many of the poems, the fragmentation of images, the fluctuations in form, the disjuncture between the linguistic sign and meaning, and the references to the historical changes in meaning foreground the contingency of "frozen" ordering systems and their dissociation from presence. The speaker is linked to those divided structures and images by his conversion into a linguistic sign; thus his predicament exactly parallels that of the forms of art and language; his image has also become fragmented and frozen. This connection between the speaker and the sign, even the speaker's explicit textuality, harks back to Carnero's own poetry, to *Dibujo de la muerte* and *El sueño de Escipión*, especially to poems like "Les Charmes de la Vie," in which the speaker's fragmented identity is linked to the loss of the classical concept of the sign as knowledge, and "El sueño de Escipión," where the history of aesthetic thought undermines the possibility of poetic unity.[22] The lyricism of *Divisibilidad indefinida* (especially notable in comparison to *Sueño*, *Variaciones*, and *Azar*) and the image of the final poem suggest a return to emotion and to some kind of spiritual wholeness, to presence, but this healing is only possible after the destruction of rationality, which was gleefully predicted in *El azar objetivo*. Despite these resounding echoes of philosophy, literature, and art, or rather because of them, *Divisibilidad indefinida* is a profoundly moving retrospection, not only of Carnero's works, but of the history of the modern self.

Afterword

I have argued in this study that Guillermo Carnero is a postmodern poet, and I have done so fully cognizant of the limitations and inconsistencies of the concept of the postmodern. Many characteristics of postmodern poetry—linguistic play, repetition, metonymic images, indeterminacy, self-consciousness, allusiveness, structural innovation—may indeed be found throughout the history of Western literature, especially in the baroque and avant-garde periods, where they imply a radical critique of social conventions. It is for this reason, perhaps, that so many critics have noted echoes of those earlier works in *novísimo* poetry.

The same critical posture toward Western culture that was considered radical in the avant-garde, however, is often deemed conservative in its present incarnation. This contradiction may be explained in terms of an inescapable historical difference between the baroque, the avant-garde, and postmodernism.[1] Spanish baroque art offered a resolution of the chaos and contradictions of the world that it reflected in an afterlife attainable only through Catholic faith and salvation. European and North American art at the beginning of the century offered at least tentative alternatives, or solutions, to an exhausted Western civilization—in the future, in the machine, in art, in the pure image, in the subconscious, or in Eastern, African, or indigenous American cultures. Even into the 1960s, the Cultural Revolution in China was hailed as an antidote to the West by the writers of *Tel Quel*. All of these images of salvation through a pure and inviolate other have proved false—at times, devastatingly so.

Postmodern literature is born of this disillusionment; in fact, one of the most important insights that links, say, Barthes, Kristeva, Heidegger, and Borges is the recognition of the limitations of that modern Western contraposition of the self and the other. It should not be surprising, then, that postmodern art is introspective and retrospective, searching for the causes and possible cures of the divisiveness in Western thought. To call this profound intellectual reevaluation of the bases of Western civilization "conservative" is itself a form of conservatism, a recourse to concepts of otherness that have had disastrous social and personal consequences.

Guillermo Carnero's poetry is intimately engaged with these issues; all of his poetry reveals and attempts to counteract the structured habits of thought and representation in modern Western civilization. The predominance of metonymy foregrounds the limitations of the metaphor (itself a metaphor for thought and history) by inviting readers to repeatedly reevaluate the image in a different context. This process also reincorporates time into the previously static image, as interpretation is textually deferred. Formal repetition has similar implications; it foregrounds the artificiality of form itself and demonstrates how repetition may result in static meanings and forms. The juxtaposition of formal repetition and metonymic and formal change, however, as in *Variaciones y figuras sobre un tema de La Bruyère*, melts those frozen forms. The use of rational language in the poems of *Variaciones y figuras* and *El azar objetivo* highlights the conventionality of poetic language, even while it suggests the irrationality of rationality itself by equating the rational with the poetic. Even the technique that has earned Carnero the label "culturalista"—the allusion to multitudinous prior works—encourages readers to review or reevaluate those works, or perhaps to seriously confront them for the first time. This technique revives frozen concepts of the works themselves, their historical context, their underlying assumptions, and even the concept of the author.

The term "culturalista" has often been applied pejoratively to Carnero's work, to imply that it is disengaged from the vital concerns of modern life. Even "postmodern," for some critics, has come to signify an absolute relativism and a subsequent inability to act. While it is certainly true that Carnero does not use everyday language and does not discuss explicitly social or political issues in his poetry, I would argue that this aesthetic difference is not inherently conservative, impersonal, or indecisive. His poetry represents a profound exploration of the historical and philosophical bases of the forms (poetic, linguistic, rational, personal) that have come to constitute Western concepts of meaning. What is more, his unmasking of authority, his critique of rationality, and his attempts to regain a sense of presence in his poetry are decisive, intellectually rigorous acts of rebellion against what he sees as the philosophical sources of personal anguish and social fragmentation.

Notes

INTRODUCTION. THE *NOVÍSIMOS*, POSTMODERNISM, AND THE POETRY OF GUILLERMO CARNERO

1. C. Christopher Soufas Jr. has discussed the aesthetic and ideological variety of this group of poets, usually referred to as the Generation of 1927, in *Conflict of Light and Wind: The Spanish Generation of 1927 and the Ideology of Poetic Form* (Middletown, Conn.: Wesleyan University Press, 1989). Significantly, from this group, the poetry of Luis Cernuda was a most significant touchstone for both Carnero and Gimferrer.

2. Several critics have argued recently that some of the poetry written by the so-called Second Postwar Generation of Spanish poets may be considered postmodern. Douglas K. Benson asserts that, to the extent that their texts are parodic, incorporate different voices, reveal their own systems of signification, and/or require readers' participation in the creation of meaning(s), Jaime Gil de Biedma, Angel González, and Gloria Fuertes are postmodernists. Margaret Persin *(Recent Spanish Poetry and the Role of the Reader* [Lewisburg, Pa.: Bucknell University Press, 1987]) and Andrew Debicki ("Poesía española de la postmodernidad," *Anales de Literatura Española* 6 [1988]: 165–80) have also studied the postmodern characteristics of these poets. Still, one could argue that Angel González and José Angel Valente, for example, do not begin to include the explicit kind of textual and linguistic play typical of *novísimo* poetry until after the first *novísimo* books were published.

3. María Nowakowska Stycos also makes the point that this reworking of modernism creates a dialogue that highlights the fact that no text is original, since each is inevitably engaged in a discourse with the past, both literary and historical. "Intertextuality in Selected Spanish Poets since 1939: Intertext/Poetics/Reader," in *After the War: Essays on Recent Spanish Poetry*, ed. Salvador Jiménez-Fajardo and John C. Wilcox (Boulder, Colo.: Society of Spanish and Spanish-American Studies, 1988), 47–54.

4. José María Castellet, *Nueve novísimos poetas españoles* (Barcelona: Barral, 1970), 43–44, 40–42.

5. Jaime Siles, "Los novísimos: La tradición como ruptura, la ruptura como tradición," *Insula* 505 (1989): 9–11.

6. César Nicolás, "Novísimos (1966-1988): Notas para una poética," *Insula* 505 (1989): 11, 13–14. The quotation is from page 13. All translations are my own.

7. Víctor García de la Concha, "La renovación estética de los años sesenta," in *El estado de las poesías,* monografía 3 of *Los Cuadernos del Norte* (Oviedo: Caja de Ahorros de Asturias, 1986), 10–22.

8. José Olivio Jiménez, "Reafirmación, proximidad, continuidad: Notas hacia la poesía española última (1975–85)," *Las Nuevas Letras* 3–4 (1985): 45.

9. José Olivio Jiménez, "Variedad y riqueza de una estética brillante," *Insula* 505 (1989): 1–2.

10. García de la Concha, "La renovación estética," 19.

11. This technique, according to Anna Balakian's recent study, *The Fiction of the Poet: From Mallarmé to the Symbolist Mode* (Princeton: Princeton University Press, 1992), is typical of symbolist and postsymbolist verse.

12. For a description of the vehement reaction to *novísimo* poetry in the anthology *Teoría y poemas* of the "Equipo Claraboya" from León, see Fanny Rubio and José Luis Falcó, *Poesía española contemporánea: Historia y antología, 1939–1980,* 2d ed. (Madrid: Alhambra, 1982), 80–81.

13. This is a New Critical view of metaphor, based upon the assumption that each term refers to an easily identified and stable reality. Semiotic critics would claim that the relationship between signifier and signified is arbitrary, that the former cannot "embody" the latter. However metaphor in modern poetry tends to be static and univocal, whereas the postmodern use of metonymy defers interpretation in time and space.

14. Guillermo Carnero, "Culturalism and 'New' Poetry. A Poem by Pedro Gimferrer: 'Cascabeles' from *Arde el mar* (1966)," trans. Frederick H. Fornoff, *Studies in Twentieth-Century Literature* 16, no. 1 (1992): 93–107.

15. See Rosa María Pereda, "Los novísimos, o la poesía de la década prodigiosa," *Los Cuadernos del Norte* 5 (1981): 59–62.

16. Rubio and Falcó, *Poesía española contemporánea,* 76.

17. Nicolás, "Novísimos," 13. Emphasis in the original.

18. Pereda, "Los novísimos," 62.

19. Castellet, *Nueve novísimos poetas españoles,* 28.

20. Ibid., 20.

21. Fanny Rubio, "De la poesía de hoy al fragmentarismo de mañana," *Revista de Occidente* 86–87 (1988): 197.

22. Luis Antonio de Villena, "Barras situacionales a una década de nuestra poesía," *Las Nuevas Letras* 3–4 (1985): 36.

23. Siles, "Los novísimos," 11.

24. Quoted in E. Martín Prado, *Nueva poesía española* (Madrid: Scorpio, 1970), 33–34.

25. Carlos Bousoño, introduction to *Ensayo de una teoría de la visión (Poesía, 1966–1977),* 2d ed., by Guillermo Carnero (Madrid: Hiperión, 1983), 26.

26. Ibid., 27. Emphasis in the original.

27. Andrew P. Debicki also makes this point in "Poesía española de la postmodernidad."

28. The concept of the generation has colored and limited the study of Spanish poetry during the twentieth century. For recent critiques of this critical convention, see Andrew P. Debicki, *Spanish Poetry of the Twentieth Century: Modernity and Beyond* (Lexington: University Press of Kentucky, 1994); Soufas, *Conflict of Light and Wind;* Philip W. Silver, *La casa de Anteo: Estudios de poética hispánica (De Antonio Machado a Claudio Rodríguez)* (Madrid: Taurus, 1985); and Jonathan Mayhew, *The Poetics of Self-Consciousness: Twentieth-Century Spanish Poetry*

(Lewisburg, Pa.: Bucknell University Press, 1994). I agree that the term "generation" has often become an exclusionary device and tends to inhibit the careful study of individual poets; however, I do believe that it is important to maintain a historical perspective. Thus, it does not make sense to call poststructuralist writers in Spain "modernist" or "symbolist."

29. Guillermo Carnero, letter to author, 9 October 1994. Luis Antonio de Villena also argues that those cultural barriers had already been broken by the end of the 1960s. "Barras situacionales."

30. As Theo D'haen explains, in postmodern paintings "the foregrounding of framing conventions shows us that what we call reality is fully as conventionally framed as what we call painting. Instead of seeing the picture in terms of its representations and referential links with so-called reality, we are now led to see that reality as preinterpreted for us by convention." "Frames and Boundaries," *Poetics Today* 10, no. 2 (1989): 433.

31. José Luis Jover, "Nueve preguntas a Guillermo Carnero (En torno a *Ensayo de una teoría de la visión*," *Nueva Estafeta* 9–10 (1979): 150.

32. Paul de Man, *Allegories of Reading: Figural Language in Rousseau, Nietzsche, Rilke, and Proust* (New Haven: Yale University Press, 1979), 151.

33. Umberto Eco, *The Role of the Reader: Explorations in the Semiotics of Texts* (Bloomington: Indiana University Press, 1979), chap. 2.

34. The difference between metaphor and metonymy has been explained and disputed by many critics, including Roman Jakobson, Gérard Genette, and Umberto Eco. As Jonathan Culler explains, Jakobson argued that metaphor was the predominant technique of poetry, since this trope strove to arrest a meaning and embody it. Metonymy, on the other hand, was more appropriate in fiction, since the various contiguous meanings could be developed over time and space (Jonathan Culler, *The Pursuit of Signs: Semiotics, Literature, Deconstruction* [Ithaca: Cornell University Press, 1981], 192). Postmodern critics have taken issue with these arguments because they are based on the questionable assumptions that the two tropes will successfully embody meaning if only used correctly and that metaphor is somehow a purer poetic device than metonymy because it can embody meaning without recourse to spatial juxtaposition (190). Most critics agree, however, that the predominance of metaphor is more typical of modern poetry, whereas metonymy is more characteristic of postmodern poetry.

35. Joseph M. Conte, *Unending Design: The Forms of Postmodern Poetry* (Ithaca: Cornell University Press, 1991), 23.

36. Geoffrey Hartman, *Criticism in the Wilderness: The Study of Literature Today* (New Haven: Yale University Press, 1980), 186.

37. Ibid., 179.

38. Geoffrey Hartman, *Saving the Text: Literature, Derrida, Philosophy* (Baltimore: Johns Hopkins University Press, 1981), xxv.

39. See especially the introduction and the first part of *Unending Design*, which discusses serial form.

40. Brian McHale, "Postmodernist Lyric and the Ontology of Poetry," *Poetics Today* 8 (1987): 19–44. The quotation is from page 29.

41. Conte, *Unending Design*, 14.

42. Jaume Pont, "Tres grupos poéticos de la inmediata posguerra: 'Garcilaso', 'Postismo', y 'Cántico' (Estética e ideología)," in *Medio siglo de cultura, 1939–1989*, ed. Manuel L. Abellán (Amsterdam: Rodopi, 1990), 79–98.

43. Conte, *Unending Design*, 15–16.

44. Luis Antonio de Villena, in fact, makes the argument that formal innovation becomes conservative when everyone imitates it. In those circumstances, a return to form is avant-garde ("Barras situacionales," 37). However, one need only think of the vastly different and innovative uses of the sonnet in the history of Spanish poetry to counter the criticism of poetic conservatism. Góngora, Sor Juana, Quevedo, Darío, and Unamuno, for example, all used the sonnet to undermine dominant concepts of order and stability.

45. Linda Hutcheon, *A Poetics of Postmodernism: History, Theory, Fiction* (New York: Routledge, 1988), 11.

46. Ibid., 57.

47. According to this view, the opponents of authoritarian regimes may be as dogmatic as the authorities they seek to topple. In fact, the vigor with which supporters of social poetry have attacked *novísimo* poetry suggests that they are, in some ways, as dogmatic as Franco.

48. Paul A. Bové, *Mastering Discourse: The Politics of Intellectual Culture* (Durham, N.C.: Duke University Press, 1992), 11.

49. Julia Kristeva, "The System and the Speaking Subject," trans. Alice Jardine, Thomas Gora and Léon S. Roudiez, in *The Kristeva Reader*, ed. Toril Moi (New York: Columbia University Press, 1986), 28.

50. As Michel Foucault argues in the first volume of *The History of Sexuality*, the purpose of repression is not to eliminate what is being repressed but to perpetuate it because power requires opposition to sustain itself (*An Introduction*, trans. Robert Hurley [New York: Vintage, 1980], 49). Therefore, rather than silencing its opponents, authority encourages them to speak because it needs sustained discourse to maintain its power.

51. For a fuller discussion of this postwar aesthetic schism, consult Jaume Pont, "Tres grupos poéticos." Carnero has also published a study of the *Cántico* group.

52. Jean-François Lyotard, *The Postmodern Condition: A Report on Knowledge*, trans. Geoff Bennington and Brian Massumi, Theory and History of Literature 10 (Minneapolis: University of Minnesota Press, 1984), 16.

53. Hutcheon, *Poetics of Postmodernism*, 11–12.

54. Lyotard, *Postmodern Condition*, xxiv.

55. Matei Calinescu, *Five Faces of Modernity: Modernism, Avant-Garde, Decadence, Kitsch, Postmodernism* (Durham, N.C.: Duke University Press, 1987), 274.

56. Richard Rorty, *Contingency, Irony, and Solidarity* (Cambridge: Cambridge University Press, 1989), xv.

57. Ibid.

58. Many critics have noted the resonance of prior aesthetic movements in Carnero's poetry, but, with the exception of Ignacio-Javier López ("Metonimia y negación: *Variaciones y figuras sobre un tema de La Bruyère* de Guillermo Carnero" *Hispanic Review* 54 [1986]: 257–77), they have not explored the implications of these echoes. César Simón, for example, notes a similarity with mannerism in the author's distance and coldness ("Un problema de asentimiento: La poesía de Guillermo Carnero," *Insula* 361 [1976]: 5); José Olivio Jiménez explains the ways in which Carnero builds on modernism ("'Estética del lujo y de la muerte': Sobre *Dibujo de la muerte* [1967], de Guillermo Carnero," *Papeles de Son Armadans* 65 [1972]: 145–57); and Clara Arranz Nicolás notes echoes of Pound and Wittgenstein in Carnero's

work ("Neopositivismo y culturalismo en la obra de Guillermo Carnero," *Cuadernos para Investigación de la Literatura Hispánica* 8 [1987]: 137–47).

59. In this sense, *Dibujo* is chaotic. As N. Katherine Hayles explains in *Chaos Bound: Orderly Disorder in Contemporary Literature and Science* (Ithaca: Cornell University Press, 1990), "Almost but not quite repeating themselves, chaotic systems generate patterns of extreme complexity, in which areas of symmetry are intermixed with asymmetry down through all scales of magnification" (10–11). Although such systems do not yield a single meaning, or one logical explanation, they are valuable and productive because they generate innumerable meanings. Given Carnero's belief that all orderly systems eventually degenerate, chaos offers the possibility of eternal recreation and renewal.

CHAPTER 1. FRAMING THE SELF IN *DIBUJO DE LA MUERTE*

1. Carnero claims that this technique is used to communicate an emotional experience while avoiding neoromantic sentimentalism. "Culturalism and 'New' Poetry. A Poem by Pedro Gimferrer: 'Cascabeles' from *Arde el mar* (1966)," trans. Frederick H. Fornoff, *Studies in Twentieth-Century Literature* 16 (1992): 97.

2. Jean-François Lyotard, *The Postmodern Condition: A Report on Knowledge*, trans. Geoff Bennington and Brian Massumi. (Minneapolis: University of Minnesota Press, 1984). The quotations are from pages 81 and 17, respectively.

3. Joseph M. Conte, *Unending Design: The Forms of Postmodern Poetry* (Ithaca: Cornell University Press, 1991), 20.

4. Julia Kristeva, "Revolution in Poetic Language," trans. Margaret Waller, in *The Kristeva Reader*, ed. Toril Moi. (New York: Columbia University Press, 1986), 111. For a summary of the current usages of the terms "intertextuality," "allusion," and "quotation," see Udo J. Hebel, "Towards a Descriptive Poetics of *Allusion*," in *Intertextuality*, ed. Heinrich F. Plett (New York: Walter de Gruyter, 1991), 135–64.

5. This use of intertextuality is specifically postmodern if "Postmodernist intertextuality is the intertextuality conceived and realized within the framework of a poststructuralist theory of intertextuality. . . . [This] means that here intertextuality is not just used as one device amongst others, but is foregrounded, displayed, thematized and theorized as a central constructional principle." Mangred Pfister, "How Postmodern is Intertextuality," in Plett, *Intertextuality*, 214.

6. I use the masculine pronoun (arbitrarily, perhaps) because all of the speakers in Carnero's poems are male.

7. In light of current literary theory and especially given the implications of this poetry, I recognize that the proper name "Guillermo Carnero" always represents a persona or a construct, be it social, literary, or critical. In this book, however, I will only set it off in quotation marks when I want to comment on the relationship between this construct, "Guillermo Carnero," and the issues of framing, representation, and the self. I deal more thoroughly with the concept of the author in the second chapter of this book.

8. "No rules of rational thought provide a vantage point from which humans can observe and know a world understood as existing independently of consciousness itself. And the self itself is de-centered, dissolving into a technological oversoul or subsumed by the

textual interplay of language." Silvio Gaggi, *Modern/Postmodern: A Study in Twentieth-Century Arts and Ideas* (Philadelphia: University of Pennsylvania Press, 1989), 159.

9. Matei Calinescu believes that the use of palinode, which he defines as "any explicit withdrawal of a statement (be it a recantation, an admission of having been mistaken, of having been a dupe, or a recognition of having lied from whatever motive, serious or playful)," is typical of postmodern texts. *Five Faces of Modernity: Modernism, Avant-Garde, Decadence, Kitsch, Postmodernism* (Durham, N.C.: Duke University Press, 1987), 309.

10. Guillermo Carnero, *Ensayo de una teoría de la visión (Poesía, 1966–1977)*, 2d ed. (Madrid: Hiperión, 1983), 77. Page numbers for *Dibujo de la muerte* that appear in the text are to this volume.

11. In *Modern/Postmodern*, Silvio Gaggi discusses at length the implications of what he calls the Pirandellian technique of meta-artistic frames. Debicki also discusses the aesthetic and temporal distance between the speaker of "Avila" and the work he describes. He notes in particular the fragmentary nature of the speaker himself and his inability—and the inability of the work—to transcend mortality. "Poesía española de la postmodernidad," *Anales de Literatura Española* 6 (1988): 177.

12. Again, the multiple framing techniques in this poetry foreground the instability of the concept of "the reader." When I use this term, I am referring to a fictional entity who, as I have explained, may be variously identified with other fictional beings or masks, such as the speaker, the poet, the other figures in the poems, "Guillermo Carnero," and "Jill Kruger-Robbins," among others. I often use the plural, "we" and "us," in my analysis of this poem because I believe that the reader comes to be identified with the speaker and the other figures of the poem; and it seems that the self is plural, although it is variably represented as singular (as "Detlev Spinell," for example). When the singular pronoun is unavoidable, I have opted for the masculine pronoun because all of the represented poetic figures have male names, but I consider the gender of the personal pronoun to be arbitrary. For further consideration of the constructed nature of gender, see Judith Butler, *Gender Trouble: Feminism and the Subversion of Identity*, (New York: Routledge, 1990).

13. David Luke, introduction to *Death in Venice and Other Stories*, by Thomas Mann (Toronto: Bantam, 1988), xxiii.

14. Ibid., xxxv.

15. This complex intertextuality with Mann's works links "Muerte en Venecia" with Mann's concerns but it does not repeat them. As we saw in "Avila," works from the past mean differently when they are framed in the present—we need only think here of Borges's "Pierre Menard, autor del Quijote." Furthermore, Mann's characters can only appear together outside of Mann's original works.

16. Ihab Hassan notes that this silence is characteristic of postmodern art. He claims that it is the result of the chain of repression in society: "[R]epression begets civilization, civilization begets more repression, more repression begets abstraction, and abstraction begets death." "The Literature of Silence," in *The Postmodern Turn: Essays in Postmodern Theory and Culture*. (Columbus: The Ohio State University Press, 1987), 18.

17. Conte, *Unending Design*, 71.

18. The connection to baroque art seems clear; one need only think of *Don Quijote* or *La vida es sueño*. A difference lies in the Catholic dogma that comes into play in the seventeenth century; in Carnero's poems, there is no such salvation.

19. Like Carnero, Watteau has been accused of frivolity because his works do not

explicitly address the political situation. However, this seeming vacuity is in itself a political statement, for Watteau began his work during the reign of Louis XIV, the absolute monarch of France who insisted that everything revolve around him. To ignore the king was thus a form of political resistance. This protest is especially evident in *L'Enseigne de Gersaint*, painted soon after the death of the Sun King, in which a portrait of Louis XIV is stored in a box while the courtesans chat among themselves, completely uninterested in the emperor's flattened and discarded presence. It is especially significant that, in this painting, the portrait of the absolute ruler is only one of a myriad of paintings in the room Watteau depicts: the world no longer revolves around the Sun King.

20. Francisco Brines has written an outstanding analysis of the relationship between the title of this poem and the poem itself ("Integración del título en el poema," *Insula* 499–500 [1988]: 52–53).

CHAPTER 2. A QUESTION OF AUTHORITY:
EL SUEÑO DE ESCIPIÓN

1. Page numbers in the text refer to Guillermo Carnero, *Ensayo de una teoría de la visión (Poesía, 1966–1977)*, 2d ed. (Madrid: Hiperión, 1983).

2. He is a subject rather than a person, formed by his speech-act. Roland Barthes, "The Death of the Author," in *The Rustle of Language*, trans. Richard Howard (Berkeley: University of California Press, 1986), 49–55.

3. This use of explanatory footnotes may constitute an allusion to T. S. Eliot's *Waste Land*, but the effect of the contradictory footnotes here more closely parallels the ways in which Borges uses them to undermine the authority of texts and their authors.

4. Jean-François Lyotard, *The Postmodern Condition: A Report on Knowledge*, trans. Geoff Bennington and Brian Massumi (Minneapolis: University of Minnesota Press, 1984), 24.

5. Science, like history and other narratives, cannot legitimize itself or other languages games because even the proof is open to challenge. Ibid., 26.

6. Again, the multiplicity of the poetic sign has ramifications for the construction of the self, although this issue is not the focus of this chapter: "[L]a universalidad de toda emoción humana hace que, dentro de su dimensión genérica, quepan muchas interpretaciones particulares, una de las cuales es la que el autor cree haber expresado para dar cuenta de su personalidad individual y única. Pero como escribimos para conocernos a nosotros mismos, y ese autoconocimiento es el que nos confiere realidad, queda siempre la angustia de la pérdida o de la deformación de esa propia realidad ante la polivalencia del texto: que él sobreviva y nosotros no" [The universality of all human emotion allows, within its generic dimension, that many individual interpretations may fit, one of these is that which the author believes to have expressed to give an accounting of his individual and unique personality. But since we write to know ourselves, and this self-knowledge is what confers reality to us, there remains always the anguish of the loss or the deformation of one's own reality against the polyvalence of the text: that it survive and not us]. Guillermo Carnero, letter to author, 24 April 1995.

7. My discussion of the author-function is based primarily on Michel Foucault's "What Is an Author?" *Textual Strategies: Perspectives in Post-Structuralist Criticism*, ed. Josué V. Harari

(Ithaca: Cornell University Press, 1979), 141–60; and on Roland Barthes, "The Death of the Author."

8. Claudio Rodríguez, *Desde mis poemas* (Madrid: Cátedra, 1983), 33.

9. José Luis Jover. "Nueve preguntas a Guillermo Carnero (En torno a *Ensayo de una teoría de la visión*)," *Nueva Estafeta* 9–10 (1979): 150.

10. This historical process is apparent even in the title of the poem, which refers to one in the pleonastic series of Scipios who sought to subdue Spain, he who placed Numancia under siege and took possession of the city's empty form following the mass suicide of its inhabitants. Even this empty victory was short-lived, since the Romans consequently lost control of Spain to a series of invaders. And, of course, Spain's center has remained unstable.

CHAPTER 3. FORMS OF REPETITION: *VARIACIONES Y FIGURAS SOBRE UN TEMA DE LA BRUYÈRE*

1. For a full study of the relationship between repetition and postmodern literature, see William V. Spanos, *Repetitions: The Postmodern Occasion in Literature and Culture* (Baton Rouge: Louisiana State University Press, 1987). Especially in chapters 3 and 5, Spanos explains how the Heideggerian concept of *logos* as a temporal act, rather than "a reified interpretation of the word *ratio* that emphasized its fixity, its centeredness, its objectness—its metaphysical possibilities" (111), translates into postmodern poetic form.

2. Ignacio-Javier López also explains the effect of lexical, structural, and syntactical repetitions in this book in his excellent essay, "Metonimia y negación: *Variaciones y figuras sobre un tema de La Bruyère* de Guillermo Carnero," *Hispanic Review* 54 (1986): 257–77. López focuses primarily on the ways in which repetition and negation undermine the transcendent quality of poetic language; I believe that Carnero's critique extends beyond poetry to all forms of linguistic expression.

3. Page numbers in the text refer to Guillermo Carnero, *Ensayo de una teoría de la visión (Poesía, 1966–1977)*, 2d ed. (Madrid: Hiperión, 1983).

4. Laura R. Scarano discusses the recurrence of negativity throughout *Ensayo de una teoría de la visión* in her article, "La poesía de Guillermo Carnero: Una estética de la negatividad," *Anales de la Literatura Española Contemporánea* 16 (1991): 321–35.

5. Joseph M. Conte, *Unending Design: The Forms of Postmodern Poetry* (Ithaca: Cornell University Press, 1991).

6. Ibid., 42.

7. Ibid.

8. Brian McHale makes the same point in "Postmodernist Lyric and the Ontology of Poetry," *Poetics Today* 8 (1987): 19–44.

CHAPTER 4. CRITICAL PARANOIA: *EL AZAR OBJETIVO*

1. Guillermo Carnero, "El juego lúgubre: La aportación de Salvador Dalí al pensamiento superrealista," in *Las armas abisinias: Ensayos sobre literatura y arte del siglo XX* (Barcelona: Anthropos, 1989), 134–67. All references to this article in the following para-

graphs will be noted parenthetically, with the page number preceded by "J". All other page numbers are to Guillermo Carnero, *Ensayo de una teoría de la visión (Poesía, 1966–1977)*, 2d ed. (Madrid: Hiperión, 1983).

2. Umberto Eco makes a similar point—avant-garde works are converted into objects of consumption in contemporary bourgeois society—in an essay on experimentalism and the avant-garde. The essay, "Experimentalismo y vanguardia" (in *La definición del arte*, trans. R. de la Iglesia [Barcelona: Ediciones Martínez Roca, 1970]), was originally published in *La Biennale* in 1962.

3. Indeed, the epigraph from Nietzsche's writings at the beginning of *El azar objetivo* indicates that he is aware of it.

4. *Variaciones y figuras sobre un tema de La Bruyère*, in contrast, foregrounds the artificiality of *poetic* language and form by incorporating "scientific" language.

5. Silvio Gaggi describes this view of language and consciousness as typically postmodern, derived from Nietzsche, Wittgenstein and Saussure: "No rules of rational thought provide a vantage point from which humans can observe and know a world understood as existing independently of consciousness itself." *Modern/Postmodern: A Study in Twentieth-Century Arts and Ideas* (Philadelphia: University of Pennsylvania Press, 1989), 159.

6. A near equivalent in English would be "unite" and "untie."

7. "Seguro" could also be translated as "safe." Both meanings come into play here, as they do at the end of the poem: as we see in all of the poems of this book, the certainty of order is attractive because it makes us feel safe, it deadens the threat of chaos.

8. Jonathan Mayhew, *The Poetics of Self-Consciousness* (Lewisburg, Pa.: Bucknell University Press, 1994), 152 n. 10.

9. Fabrizio Carini Motta (1627–99) designed the stage and theater seating according to precise mathematical calculations so as to allow maximum visibility to the audience, and he also perfected theatrical machinery to add to the fantasy of theater. For more information, please consult the study and translation by Orville K. Larson, *The Theatrical Writings of Fabrizio Carini Motta* (Carbondale: Southern Illinois University Press, 1987).

10. "Fabrizio" is therefore clearly related to the "Dalí" of "El juego lúgubre" in that he must be "cosificado," reified, in order to be manipulated. The effect of the poem resembles Carnero's objective in the essay: "descosificación."

11. Matei Calinescu discusses the critical differences between the avant-garde and the postmodern in *Five Faces of Modernity: Modernism, Avant-Garde, Decadence, Kitsch, Postmodern* (Durham, N.C.: Duke University Press, 1987).

CHAPTER 5. IN RETROSPECT: *DIVISIBILIDAD INDEFINIDA*

1. The question arises as to the relationship between these new poetics and their context. According to Luis Antonio de Villena, Franco's death had no effect whatsoever on Spanish poetry, for *novísimo* poetry had already broken cultural frontiers by including allusions to international authors and to the mass media ("Barras situacionales a una década de nuestra poesía," *Las Nuevas Letras* 3–4 [1985]: 36). One is tempted to seek some explanation for the dramatic change in poetics in the massive upheavals of post-Franco society, but such generalizations are risky, since they may be based on a false concept of causality.

2. As Jonathan Mayhew states, "eclecticism itself is taken to be a 'generational'

signpost." *The Poetics of Self-Consciousness: Twentieth-Century Spanish Poetry* (Lewisburg, Pa.: Bucknell University Press, 1994), 131.

3. Amparo Amorós, "¡Los novísimos y cierra España! Reflexión crítica sobre algunos fenómenos estéticos que configuran la poesía de los años ochenta," *Insula* 512–13 (1989): 65. Emphasis in the original.

4. Ibid., 66.

5. Carnero presents this idea in "La corte de los poetas: Los últimos veinte años de poesía española en castellano," *Revista de Occidente* 23 (1983): 43-59. The quotation is from Amorós, "¡Los novísimos y cierra España!," 66.

6. César Nicolás. "Novísimos (1966–1988): Notas para una poética," *Insula* 505 (1989): 14.

7. Ibid.

8. Ibid., 13.

9. Guillermo Carnero, "Dad limosna a Belisario," in *Ensayo de una teoría de la visión (Poesía, 1966–1977)*, 2d ed. (Madrid: Hiperión, 1983), 173.

10. Jaime Giordano also notes this retrospection in his review of *Divisibilidad indefinida*. He also cites the allusions to Darío and Neruda and the irony of the book, which he sees as an exploration of vanity. Review of *Divisibilidad indefinida*, *España Contemporánea* 5, no. 1 (1992): 122–24.

11. Page numbers in the text refer to *Divisibilidad indefinida, 1979–1989* (Madrid: Renacimiento, 1990).

12. The first eight lines of the *Libro de Alexandre* "se consideran el manifiesto de la poesía superculta de la época, culta por contraste con la de los autores de los cantares de gesta" [are considered the manifesto of the supercultured poetry of the period, cultured in contrast to that of the authors of the oral ballads], Guillermo Carnero, letter to author, 9 October 1994.

13. The use of the sonnet form in conjunction with unstructured poems recalls the relationship between metaphor and metonymy in *Dibujo de la muerte*.

14. For a full analysis of the Western concept of the self, consult Charles Taylor, *Sources of the Self: The Making of Modern Identity* (Cambridge: Harvard University Press, 1989). For more insight on the historicity of the lyric, see Mark Jeffreys, "Ideologies of Lyric: A Problem of Genre in Contemporary Anglophone Poetics," *PMLA* 110 (1995): 196–205, and Marjorie Perloff, *The Dance of the Intellect: Studies in the Poetry of the Pound Tradition* (New York: Cambridge University Press, 1985). Paul Jay discusses the autobiographical mode in *Being in the Text: Self-Representation from Wordsworth to Roland Barthes* (Ithaca: Cornell University Press, 1984), as does Laura Marcus, *Auto/biographical Discourses: Theory, Criticism, Practice* (Manchester: Manchester University Press, 1994).

15. This problem of presence and absence clearly recalls the poem "Elogio de la dialéctica a la manera de Magritte" from *El azar objetivo*.

16. Roland Barthes, *Elements of Semiology*, trans. Annette Lavers and Colin Smith (New York: Hill and Wang, 1967), 64.

17. The concepts of the self that I discuss in the following paragraphs are based upon Taylor's study *Sources of the Self*.

18. The use of the masculine "man," rather than the neutral "humanity" or "humankind," is appropriate, I believe, in this historical context.

19. One can easily visualize here the figure of a classical or neoclassical sculpture. In

fact, many of the poems of *Divisibilidad indefinida* have this visual quality, evoking, for example, landscapes from Yves Tanguy, who appears in an epigraph, or Salvador Dalí, whose painting *The Persistence of Memory* repeatedly comes to mind, or Fortunato Depero, whose *Ciudad mecanizada por la luna* appears at the end of "Los motivos del jardín" (I am grateful to Guillermo Carnero for this final observation). I have opted to study Carnero's book in the context of a literary and philosophical history; it would be interesting to analyze it as well in the context of the visual arts.

20. This poem brings to mind two baroque sonnets—Góngora's "Mientras por competir con tu cabello" and Sor Juana's "Este que ves"—and indeed there are reflections of baroque techniques and themes throughout Carnero's poetry. In comparison to the baroque sonnets I mention, Carnero's poem does not point to a possible salvation from nothingness through religious faith.

21. This critique recalls "La busca de la certeza" from *El azar objetivo*.

22. Michel Foucault analyzes the relationship between the sign, identity, and knowledge in "Representing," chapter 3 of *The Order of Things: An Archaeology of the Human Sciences*, ed. R. D. Laing (New York: Vintage, 1973).

Afterword

1. Here, I agree with Matei Calinescu's view that the postmodern must be seen in its historical context; it cannot be reduced to a list of techniques (*Five Faces of Modernity: Modernism, Avant-Garde, Decadence, Kitsch, Postmodernism* [Durham, N.C.: Duke University Press, 1987], 307). To categorize postmodern works on a purely formal basis in fact runs counter to the texts themselves, which seek to reincorporate time, historicity, into the process of interpretation.

Bibliography

Amorós, Amparo. "¡Los novísimos y cierra España! Reflexión crítica sobre algunos fenómenos estéticos que configuran la poesía de los años ochenta." *Insula* 512–13 (1989): 63–67.

Andres, Glenn, John M. Hunisak, and A. Richard Turner. *The Art of Florence*. 2 vols. New York: Abbeville, 1988.

Arranz Nicolás, Clara. "Neopositivismo y culturalismo en la obra de Guillermo Carnero." *Cuadernos para Investigación de la Literatura Hispánica* 8 (1987): 137–47.

Balakian, Anna. *The Fiction of the Poet: From Mallarmé to the Symbolist Mode*. Princeton: Princeton University Press, 1992.

Barthes, Roland. "The Death of the Author." In *The Rustle of Language*, translated by Richard Howard, 49–55. Berkeley: University of California Press, 1989.

———. *Elements of Semiology*. Translated by Annette Lavers and Colin Smith. New York: Hill and Wang, 1967.

Benson, Douglas K. "Tres calillas en la posmodernidad y la poesía española contemporánea." *Siglo XX/Twentieth Century* 12, nos. 1–2 (1994): 69–85.

Bousoño, Carlos. Introduction to *Ensayo de una teoría de la visión*, 2d ed., by Guillermo Carnero. Madrid: Hiperión, 1983.

———. *Poesía poscontemporánea: Cuatro estudios y una introducción*. Madrid: Júcar, 1984.

Bové, Paul A. *Mastering Discourse: The Politics of Intellectual Culture*. Durham, N.C.: Duke University Press, 1992.

Brines, Francisco. "Integración del título en el poema." *Insula* 499–500 (1988): 52–53.

Calinescu, Matei. *Five Faces of Modernity: Modernism, Avant-Garde, Decadence, Kitsch, Postmodernism*. Durham, N.C.: Duke University Press, 1987.

Camandone de Cohen, Mirta. "Asedio a la poesía de Guillermo Carnero." *Hispanic Journal* 7 (1985): 123–29.

Cañas, Dionisio. "El sujeto poético posmoderno." *Insula* 512–13 (1989): 52–53.

Carini Motta, Fabrizio. *The Theatrical Writings of Fabrizio Carini Motta: Translations of "Trattato sopra la struttura de'Theatri e scene," 1676 and "Costruzione de teatri e machini teatrali," 1688*. Translated and with an introduction by Orville K. Larson. Carbondale: Southern Illinois University Press, 1987.

Carnero, Guillermo. "Cuarenta años de poesía española." *Insula* 502 (1988): 10.

———. "Culturalism and 'New' Poetry. A Poem by Pedro Gimferrer: 'Cascabeles' from *Arde el mar* (1966)." Translated by Frederick H. Fornoff. *Studies in Twentieth-Century Literature* 16, no. 1 (1992): 93–107.

———. *Divisibilidad indefinida, 1979–1989*. Madrid: Renacimiento, 1990. All references for the poems of *Divisibilidad indefinida* are to this volume.

———. "El juego lúgubre: La aportación de Salvador Dalí al pensamiento surrealista." In *Las armas abisinias: Ensayos sobre literatura y arte del siglo XX*, 134–67. Barcelona: Anthropos, 1989.

———. *Ensayo de una teoría de la visión (Poesía, 1966–1977)*. 2d ed. Madrid: Hiperión, 1983. All references for the poems of *Dibujo de la muerte, El sueño de Escipión, Variaciones y figuras sobre un tema de La Bruyère*, and *El azar objetivo* are to this volume.

———. "Extremos a que ha llegado la literatura europea." *Camp de l'arpa* 23–24 (1975): 36–38.

———. "La corte de los poetas: Los últimos veinte años de poesía española en castellano." *Revista de Occidente* 23 (1983): 43–59.

———. "Pedro Montengón (1745–1824): Un poeta entre dos siglos." *Hispanic Review* 59 (1991): 125–41.

Casado, Miguel. "Líneas de los 'novísimos.'" *Revista de Occidente* 86–87 (1988): 204–24.

Castellet, José María. *Nueve novísimos poetas españoles*. Barcelona: Barral, 1970.

Cismaru, Alfred. *Boris Vian*. New York: Twayne, 1974.

Colinas, Antonio. "El método y el azar." *Camp de l'arpa* 23–24 (1975): 41.

———. "Notas para una poética de nuestro tiempo." *Insula* 293 (1971): 1, 12.

Conte, Joseph M. *Unending Design: The Forms of Postmodern Poetry*. Ithaca: Cornell University Press, 1991.

Culler, Jonathan. *The Pursuit of Signs: Semiotics, Literature, Deconstruction*. Ithaca: Cornell University Press, 1981.

Darío, Rubén. "Yo soy aquel." In *Antología poética*, edited by Guillermo de Torre, 73–77. 4th ed. Buenos Aires: Losada, 1976.

Debicki, Andrew P. "La poesía postmoderna de los novísimos: Una nueva postura ante la realidad y el arte." *Insula* 505 (1989): 15–16.

———. "New Poets, New Works, New Approaches: Recent Spanish Poetry." *Siglo XX/Twentieth Century* 8 (1990–91): 41–53.

———. "Poesía española de la postmodernidad." *Anales de Literatura Española* 6 (1988): 165–80.

———. "A Poetics and a Poetry of Indeterminacy: Recent Spanish Poetry." Paper delivered at the MLA Convention, 29 December 1989, San Francisco.

———. *Spanish Poetry of the Twentieth Century: Modernity and Beyond*. Lexington: University Press of Kentucky, 1994.

———. "Una poesía de la postmodernidad: Los novísimos." *Anales de la Literatura Española Contemporánea* 14, no. 1–3 (1989): 33–50.

de Man, Paul. *Allegories of Reading: Figural Language in Rousseau, Nietzsche, Rilke, and Proust*. New Haven: Yale University Press, 1979.

D'haen, Theo. "Frames and Boundaries." *Poetics Today* 10, no. 2 (1989): 429–38.

Dietz, Bernd. "El postismo y su lugar en la poesía española contemporánea." *Insula* 510 (1989): 9.

Eco, Umberto. "Experimentalismo y vanguardia." In *La definición del arte*, translated by R. de la Iglesia. Barcelona: Ediciones Martínez Roca, 1970.

———. *The Role of the Reader: Explorations in the Semiotics of Texts*. Bloomington: Indiana University Press, 1979.

Foucault, Michel. *An Introduction*. Vol. 1 of *The History of Sexuality*. Translated by Robert Hurley. 3 vols. New York: Vintage, 1980.

———. *The Care of the Self*. Vol. 3 of *The History of Sexuality*. Translated by Robert Hurley. 3 vols. New York: Pantheon, 1986.

———. *The Order of Things: An Archaeology of the Human Sciences*. Edited by R. D. Laing. New York: Vintage, 1973.

———. *Power/Knowledge: Selected Interviews and Other Writings, 1972–1977*. Translated by Colin Gordon, Leo Marshall, John Mepham, and Kate Soper. Edited by Colin Gordon. New York: Pantheon, 1980.

———. *The Use of Pleasure*. Vol. 2 of *The History of Sexuality*. Translated by Robert Hurley. 3 vols. New York: Vintage, 1986.

———. "What Is an Author?" In *Textual Strategies: Perspectives in Post-Structuralist Criticism*, edited by Josué V. Harari, 141–60. Ithaca: Cornell University Press, 1979.

Gaggi, Silvio. *Modern/Postmodern: A Study in Twentieth-Century Arts and Ideas*. Philadelphia: University of Pennsylvania Press, 1989.

García Berrio, Antonio. "El imaginario cultural en la estética de los 'novísimos.'" *Insula* 508 (1989): 13–15.

García de la Concha, Víctor. "La renovación estética de los años sesenta." In *"El estado de las poesías."* Monografía 3. *Los Cuadernos del Norte*, 10–22. Oviedo: Caja de Ahorros de Asturias, 1986.

Giordano, Jaime. Review of *Divisibilidad indefinida*, by Guillermo Carnero. *España Contemporánea* 5, no. 1 (1992): 122–24.

González, Shirley Mangini. "Entre la experiencia y la revelación: La metapoesía en la España de posguerra." *Anales de la Literatura Española Contemporánea* 10, nos. 1–3 (1985): 31–40.

Handelman, Susan A. *The Slayers of Moses: The Emergence of Rabbinic Interpretation in Modern Literary Theory*. Albany: State University of New York Press, 1982.

Hartman, Geoffrey. *Criticism in the Wilderness: The Study of Literature Today*. New Haven: Yale University Press, 1980.

———. *Saving the Text: Literature, Derrida, Philosophy*. Baltimore: Johns Hopkins University Press, 1981.

Hassan, Ihab. "The Literature of Silence." In *The Postmodern Turn: Essays in Postmodern Theory and Culture*, 3–22. Columbus: The Ohio State University Press, 1987.

Hayles, N. Catherine. *Chaos Bound: Orderly Disorder in Contemporary Literature and Science*. Ithaca: Cornell University Press, 1990.

Hebel, Udo J. "Towards a Descriptive Poetics of *Allusion*." In *Intertextuality*, edited by Heinrich F. Plett, 135–64. New York: Walter de Gruyter, 1991.

Hutcheon, Linda. *A Poetics of Postmodernism: History, Theory, Fiction*. New York: Routledge, 1988.

Ilie, Paul. "The Disguises of Protest: Contemporary Spanish Poetry." *Michigan Quarterly Review* 10 (1971): 38–48.

Jay, Paul. *Being in the Text: Self-Representation from Wordsworth to Roland Barthes*. Ithaca: Cornell University Press, 1984.

Jeffreys, Mark. "Ideologies of Lyric: A Problem of Genre in Contemporary Anglophone Poetics." *PMLA* 110 (1995): 196–205.

Jiménez, José Olivio. "'Estética del lujo y de la muerte': Sobre *Dibujo de la muerte* (1967), de Guillermo Carnero." *Papeles de Son Armadans* 65 (1972): 145–57.

———. "Reafirmación, proximidad, continuidad: Notas hacia la poesía española última (1975-85)." *Las Nuevas Letras* 3–4 (1985): 40–48.

———. "Variedad y riqueza de una estética brillante." *Insula* 505 (1989): 1–2.

Jover, José Luis. "Nueve preguntas a Guillermo Carnero (En torno a *Ensayo de una teoría de la visión*)." *Nueva Estafeta* 9–10 (1979): 148–53.

Kristeva, Julia. "Revolution in Poetic Language." Translated by Margaret Waller. In *The Kristeva Reader*, edited by Toril Moi, 89–136. New York: Columbia University Press, 1986.

———. "The System and the Speaking Subject." Translated by Alice Jardine, Thomas Gora, and Léon S. Roudiez. In *The Kristeva Reader*, edited by Toril Moi, 24–61. New York: Columbia University Press, 1986.

López, Ignacio-Javier. "El silencio y la piedra: Metáforas de la tradición en la poesía española contemporánea." *Bulletin of Hispanic Studies* 67 (1990): 43–56.

———. "Metonimia y negación: *Variaciones y figuras sobre un tema de La Bruyère* de Guillermo Carnero." *Hispanic Review* 54 (1986): 257–77.

López de Abiada, José M. "Los novísimos en la última encuesta sobre poesía española contemporánea." *Insula* 505 (1989): 18–19.

Luke, David. Introduction to *Death in Venice and Other Stories*, by Thomas Mann. Toronto: Bantam, 1988.

Lyotard, Jean-François. *The Postmodern Condition: A Report on Knowledge*. Translated by Geoff Bennington and Brian Massumi. Minneapolis: University of Minnesota Press, 1984.

Mann, Thomas. *Death in Venice*. In *Death in Venice and Other Stories*, translated by David Luke, 195–263. Toronto: Bantam, 1988.

———. *The Magic Mountain*. Translated by H. T. Lowe-Porter. New York: Vintage, 1969.

———. *Tristan*. In *Death in Venice and Other Stories*, translated by David Luke, 93–132. Toronto: Bantam, 1988.

Marcus, Laura. *Auto/biographical Discourses: Theory, Criticism, Practice*. Manchester: Manchester University Press, 1994.

Martín, Salustiano. "La teoría de la visión de Guillermo Carnero." *Insula* 404–5 (1980): 24.

Martín Prado, E. *Nueva poesía española*. Madrid: Scorpio, 1970.

Mayhew, Jonathan. *Claudio Rodríguez and the Language of Poetic Vision*. Lewisburg, Pa.: Bucknell University Press, 1990.

———. *The Poetics of Self-Consciousness: Twentieth-Century Spanish Poetry*. Lewisburg, Pa.: Bucknell University Press, 1994.

McHale, Brian. "Postmodernist Lyric and the Ontology of Poetry." *Poetics Today* 8 (1987): 19–44.

Nicolás, César. "Novísimos (1966–1988): Notas para una poética." *Insula* 505 (1989): 11, 13–14.

Pereda, Rosa María. "Los novísimos, o la poesía de la década prodigiosa." *Los Cuadernos del Norte* 5 (1981): 59–62.

Perloff, Marjorie. *The Dance of the Intellect: Studies in the Poetry of the Pound Tradition.* New York: Cambridge University Press, 1985.

———. *Postmodern Genres.* Norman: University of Oklahoma Press, 1989.

Persin, Margaret H. *Recent Spanish Poetry and the Role of the Reader.* Lewisburg, Pa.: Bucknell University Press, 1987.

Persin, Margaret H., Andrew P. Debicki, Nancy Mandlove, and Robert C. Spires. "Metaliterature and Recent Spanish Literature." *Revista Canadiense de Estudios Hispánicos* 7 (1983): 297–309.

Pfister, Mangred. "How Postmodern is Intertextuality?" In *Intertextuality*, edited by Heinrich F. Plett, 207–24. New York: Walter de Gruyter, 1991.

Piera, José. "Los lúcidos fantasmas de Guillermo Carnero." *Camp de l'arpa* 14 (1974): 18–20.

Plato. *The Dialogues of Plato.* Translated by Benjamin Jowett. Chicago: Encyclopaedia Britannica, 1952.

Pont, Jaume. "Tres grupos poéticos de la inmediata posguerra: 'Garcilaso', 'Postismo', y 'Cántico' (Estética e ideología)." In *Medio siglo de cultura, 1939–1989*, edited by Manuel L. Abellán, 79–98. Dialogos Hispánicos de Amsterdam 9. Amsterdam: Rodopi, 1990.

Ramos, Juan Luis. "Meditación sobre las contrariedades del azar (Acerca de la poesía de Guillermo Carnero)." *I & L* 1 (1985): 207–16.

Rodríguez, Claudio. *Don de la ebriedad.* In *Desde mis poemas*, 33–63. Madrid: Cátedra, 1983.

Rorty, Richard. *Contingency, Irony, and Solidarity.* Cambridge: Cambridge University Press, 1989.

Rubio, Fanny. "Apostilla para los poetas del presente." *Insula* 512–13 (1989): 51–52.

———. "De la poesía de hoy al fragmentarismo de mañana." *Revista de Occidente* 86–87 (1988): 195–203.

Rubio, Fanny, and José Luis Falcó. *Poesía española contemporánea: Historia y antología, 1939–1980.* 2d ed. Madrid: Alhambra, 1982.

Salinas, Pedro. "Livia Schubert, incompleta." *Víspera del gozo.* Madrid: Alianza, 1974.

Sánchez Robayna, Andrés. "Situación de la poesía." *Revista de Occidente* 86–87 (1988): 225–30.

Scarano, Laura. "La poesía de Guillermo Carnero: Una estética de la negatividad." *Anales de la Literatura Española Contemporánea* 16 (1991): 321–35.

Siles, Jaime. "Los novísimos: La tradición como ruptura, la ruptura como tradición." *Insula* 505 (1989): 9–11.

Silver, Philip W. *La casa de Anteo: Estudios de poética hispánica (De Antonio Machado a Claudio Rodríguez).* Madrid: Taurus, 1985.

Simón, César. "Fracaso y triunfo del lenguaje en Guillermo Carnero." *Papeles de Son Armadans* 83 (1976): 249–63.

---. "Un problema de asentimiento: La poesía de Guillermo Carnero." *Insula* 361 (1976): 5.

Soufas, C. Christopher, Jr. *Conflict of Light and Wind: The Spanish Generation of 1927 and the Ideology of Poetic Form.* Middletown, Conn.: Wesleyan University Press, 1989.

Spanos, William V. *Repetitions: The Postmodern Occasion in Literature and Culture.* Baton Rouge: Louisiana State University Press, 1987.

Stycos, María Nowakowska. "Intertextuality in Selected Spanish Poets since 1939: Intertext/Poetics/Reader." In *After the War: Essays on Recent Spanish Poetry*, edited by Salvador Jiménez-Fajardo and John C. Wilcox, 47–54. Boulder, Colo.: Society of Spanish and Spanish-American Studies, 1988.

Talens, Jenaro. "La coartada metapoética." *Insula* 512–13 (1989): 55–57.

Taylor, Charles. *Sources of the Self: The Making of Modern Identity.* Cambridge: Harvard University Press, 1989.

van Alphen, Ernst. "The Heterotopian Space of the Discussions on Postmodernism." *Poetics Today* 10 (1989): 819–39.

Villena, Luis Antonio de. "Barras situacionales a una década de nuestra poesía." *Las Nuevas Letras* 3–4 (1985): 36–38.

Index

Alvarez, José María, 14, 15
Amorós, Amparo, 116, 146nn.. 3, 4, and 5
Anacreon (Anacreonte), 47, 48, 49
analogous historical personage, 29, 49
Arranz Nicolás, Clara, 140–41n. 58
author: and allusion, 53, 60; author-function, 54; and authority, 23, 26, 43, 47, 52, 53, 59–60, 66, 67, 69–71, 73–75; death of, 54; and ordering systems, 23, 27; and the reader, 26, 30, 31, 35, 42, 47, 52–55, 58–59, 66–67, 142 n. 12; and the referent, 31, 42, 47, 48, 56, 61–62, 63–65; and the self, 23, 35, 41–42; and sociohistorical context, 31, 33, 35, 48–49, 74; and the text, 27, 30, 42–43, 48, 56, 59, 73, 143n. 6; and transcendence, 31, 41, 142n. 11
avant-garde, 80, 95–98, 115, 135, 145 nn. 2 and 11
Azúa, Félix de, 14, 15, 117

Balakian, Anna, 138n. 11
Barnatán, Marco Ricardo, 15
baroque, 16, 25, 73, 135, 142n. 18, 147 n. 20
Barthes, Roland, 20, 121, 135, 143n. 2, 143–44n. 7
Baudelaire, Charles, 62
Benson, Douglas K., 137n. 2
Borges, Jorge Luis, 91, 92, 135, 142n. 15, 143n. 3

Bousoño, Carlos, 13, 18–19
Bové, Paul A., 23
Brines, Francisco, 143n. 20
Butler, Judith, 142n. 12

Calinescu, Matei, 25, 142n. 9, 145n. 11, 147n. 1
Cántico, 13, 24, 139nn. 42 and 51
Careggi, 72–73
Carnero, Guillermo: "El altísimo Juan Sforza compone unos loores a su dama mientras César Borgia marcha sobre Pésaro," 49, 143n. 20; "Avila," 32–35, 142nn. 11 and 15; "El azar objetivo," 113–14; "La busca de la certeza," 100–101, 147n. 21; "Catedral de Avila," 119; "Chagrin d'amour, principe d'oeuvre d'art," 53, 59–67, 74; "Les Charmes de la Vie," 43–49, 121, 134; "Convento de Santo Tomé," 119, 127–28; "Dad limosna a Belisario," 89, 91, 118; "De la inutilidad de los cristales ópticos," 112–13; "Discurso del método," 76–77, 78–80, 98; "Divisibilidad indefinida," 119, 130–32; "Domus áurea," 80–87; "Elogio de la dialéctica a la manera de Magritte," 104–9; "L'enigme de l'heure," 93–94; "Erótica del marabú," 52, 53, 54–56; "Eupalinos," 109–12; "Fantasía de un

155

Carnero, Guillermo *(continued):*
  amanecer de invierno," 119, 129;
  "La hacedora de lluvia," 122, 132–34;
  "Ineptitud de Orfeo y alabanza de
  Alceste," 52, 53; "Investigación de una
  doble metonimia," 53, 56–59, 121;
  "Jardín inglés," 52, 53, 59, 74, 129;
  "El juego lúgubre," 95–98, 114–15;
  "Lección del agua," 128–29; "Lección
  del páramo," 119, 120–23; "La
  meditación de la pecera," 101–4;
  "Mira el breve minuto de la rosa," 91–
  92; "Los motivos del jardín," 119,
  129–30; "Muerte en Venecia," 35–43,
  121, 142n. 15; "Museo de historia
  natural," 99–100; "Música para fuegos
  de artificio," 119, 123–26; "Palabras
  de Tersites," 90–91; "Queluz," 87–88;
  "Rodéanos de rápidos desnudos," 52,
  53; "Sotheby's," 88–90; "El sueño de
  Escipión," 51, 67–74, 134
Carini Motta, Fabrizio, 110, 145n. 9
Carrillo y Sotomayor, Luis, 60
Castellet, José María, 14, 15, 17
Cavalcanti, 67
Colinas, Antonio, 14, 15
Conte, Joseph M., 21, 22, 23, 30, 43, 78, 139n. 39
Cuenca, Luis Alberto de, 15
Culler, Jonathan, 139n. 34

Dalí, Salvador, 95–99, 100, 114–15, 145 n. 10, 146–47n. 19
Darío, Rubén, 27, 123, 126, 140n. 44, 146n. 10
Debicki, Andrew P., 19, 137n. 2, 138 nn. 27 and 28, 142n. 11
de Man, Paul, 21
Depero, Fortunato, 146–47n. 19
D'haen, Theo, 139n. 30

Eco, Umberto, 21, 145n. 2
Eliot, T. S., 27, 122–23, 143n. 3

Fabrizio, 109–11, 112, 145n. 9

Falcó, José Luis, 138n. 12
Ficino, Marcilio, 60, 63, 72
Foucault, Michel, 20, 54, 56, 140n. 50, 143n. 7, 147n. 22
Franco, Francisco, 13, 16, 18, 19, 22, 29, 74, 116, 140n. 47, 145n. 1

Gaggi, Silvio, 141–42n. 8, 142n. 11, 145 n. 5
García de la Concha, Víctor, 15, 16
Garcilaso, 23, 24, 139n. 42
Garcilaso de la Vega, 27, 122
Gil de Biedma, Jaime, 13, 137n. 2
Gimferrer, Pere (Pedro), 14, 15, 18, 117, 137n. 1, 141n. 1
Giordano, Jaime, 146n. 10
Góngora, 60, 140n. 44, 147n. 20
González, Angel, 137n. 2
Guillén, Jorge, 27, 131

Handel, 123, 126
Hartman, Geoffrey, 21–22
Hassan, Ihab, 142n. 16
Hayles, N. Catherine, 141n. 59
Heidegger, Martin, 20, 122, 135, 144n. 1
Homer, 91; *Iliad*, 90–91
Hutcheon, Linda, 23, 24, 140nn. 45, 46, and 53

intertextuality: and authority, 21, 26, 53–54, 60, 62–63, 67–70, 73–74; definition of, 30–31, 141n. 4; and elitism, 16, 29; and the linguistic sign, 41, 122; and meaning, 20, 25, 41, 68–74; and ordering systems, 21, 118; and originality, 41, 69; and postmodernism, 14, 20, 141n. 5; and the reader, 34, 42–43, 53–54, 72; and the self, 26, 35, 41–42, 123, 126; and sociohistorical context, 31, 34, 43, 74; and transcendence, 21, 25, 26, 30, 41, 62–63

Jay, Paul, 146n. 14
Jeffreys, Mark, 146n. 14

Jiménez, José Olivio, 15, 140n. 58
Jiménez, Juan Ramón, 27, 131
Jover, José Luis, 20

Kristeva, Julia, 23, 30–31, 135

La Bruyère, 77, 78
Laforgue, Jules, 68, 72, 73
Libro de Alexandre, 27, 118, 146n. 12
López, Ignacio-Javier, 140n. 58, 144n. 2
Lyotard, Jean-François, 24, 30, 53

Magritte, René, 104–5, 108–9
Mallarmé, Stéphane, 71
Mann, Thomas, 36, 38, 39, 41–42, 49, 142n. 15
Marcus, Laura, 146n. 14
Martínez Sarrión, Antonio, 14, 15
Mayhew, Jonathan, 110, 138–39n. 28, 145–46n. 2
McHale, Brian, 22, 144n. 8
metaphor, 16, 21–22, 25, 80, 82–83, 89, 136, 138n. 13, 139n. 34, 146n. 13
metapoetry, 13, 14, 15, 17, 19, 20, 23, 26, 35, 51–56, 59, 65–67, 74
metonymy: and allusion, 21, 26, 30–31, 49, 51–53, 91; and metaphor, 16, 21, 25, 83, 139n. 34; and ordering systems (conceptual, linguistic, personal, political, or social), 22, 25, 26, 32, 49, 58–59, 77, 105, 110, 136; and poetic form, 21, 43, 58–59, 78; and postmodernism, 20, 21, 22, 135, 138 n. 13, 139n. 34
modernism, 13, 16, 30, 137n. 3, 138n. 13, 139n. 34
Moix, Ana María, 14
Molina-Foix, Vicente, 14

Neoplatonism, 59, 60, 66, 73, 119, 122
Nicolás, César, 14–15, 17, 117
Nietzsche, Friedrich, 98, 99, 100, 101, 145nn. 3 and 5
novísimo poetry: critiques of, 16–17; definitions of, 14–16; and postmodernism, 13–14, 15, 19–25; as social criticism, 17–25

objective chance, 95–96, 114

palinode, 32, 77, 142n. 9
Panero, Leopoldo María, 14, 15, 117
paranoiac-critical method, 95–99, 114–15
Pereda, Rosa María, 16, 17
Perloff, Marjorie, 146n. 14
Persin, Margaret, 137n. 2
Pico de Mirandola, 72–73
Plato, 60, 63, 72, 99, 105. *See also* Neoplatonism
poetic form, 21, 22, 23, 30, 43, 76, 78–80, 86–87, 91, 92–93, 116, 117, 118–19, 122, 128–29, 134, 136, 139n. 39, 140n. 44, 146n. 13
Pont, Jaume, 139n. 42 (23), 140n. 51
posnovísimos, 116–17, 145nn. 1 and 2
Postismo, 13, 24, 139n. 42
postmodernism, 135–36, 145n. 5, 147n. 1; and the avant-garde, 98–99, 114–15, 145n. 11; and intertextuality, 141n. 5; and painting, 139n. 30; and palinode, 142n. 9; and poetry, 20–25, 30, 43, 77–78, 138n. 13, 139n. 34, 144n. 1; and repetition, 76–78; and silence, 16; in Spain 14–20, 137n. 2

Ravi, Bison. *See* Vian, Boris.
reader. *See* author, and the reader; intertextuality, and the reader
Renaissance, 60, 63, 119, 122, 129
Rodríguez, Claudio, 13, 62, 66
Rorty, Richard, 25
Rubio, Fanny, 17–18, 138n. 12

Salinas, Pedro, 91
Scarano, Laura, 144n. 4
science: and authority, 53, 70; and chaos, 141n. 59; and irrationality, 102; and order, 70; and proof, 53; and rationality, 98, 101

scientific discourse: and poetic discourse, 79–80, 98, 101, 145 n. 4
self: and intertextuality, 120; and the linguistic sign, 119–20, 121–22, 124–26, 129–31, 134; and philosophy, 118, 122, 126–27; and poetic form, 119, 122–23, 129, 134; and the poetic image, 121, 123, 127–28, 130–31, 134
Shakespeare, William, 68, 70, 72, 73
silence, 32, 33, 41, 49, 116–17, 130, 142 n. 16
Siles, Jaime, 14, 15, 17, 18, 117
Silver, Philip W., 138 n. 28
Simón, César, 140 n. 58
social poetry, 24, 29
Soufas, C. Christopher, Jr., 137 n. 1, 138 n. 28
Spanos, William V., 144 n. 1
speaker. *See* author; self
Stycos, María Nowakowska, 137 n. 3

surrealism, 14, 15, 95–99, 115. *See also* avant-garde
symbolism, 25, 30, 73, 80, 138 n. 11

Talens, Jenaro, 14, 15, 17
Tanguy, Yves, 146–47 n. 19
Taylor, Charles, 146 nn. 14 and 17
Tel Quel, 20, 135

Ullán, José Miguel, 14, 15, 117
Unamuno, Miguel de, 140 n. 44

Valente, José Angel, 13, 137 n. 2
Valéry, Paul, 111
Vázquez Montalbán, Manuel, 14
Vian, Boris, 67, 69, 72, 74
Villena, Luis Antonio de, 14, 15, 18, 139 n. 29, 140 n. 44

Watteau, 29, 31, 43, 46, 47, 49, 50, 142–43 n. 19
Wittgenstein, 99, 140–41 n. 58, 145 n. 5